GARY THOMAS

WITH KEVIN AND SHERRY HARNEY

SACRED MARRIAGE

*What If God Designed Marriage to
Make Us Holy More Than to Make Us Happy?*

REVISED & UPDATED

Sacred Marriage Bible Study Guide (Revised and Updated)
© 2025 by Gary Thomas

Published in Grand Rapids, Michigan, by HarperChristian Resources. HarperChristian Resources is a registered trademark of HarperCollins Christian Publishing, Inc.

Requests for information should be sent to customercare@harpercollins.com.

ISBN 978-0-310-17372-4 (softcover)
ISBN 978-0-310-17373-1 (ebook)

All Scripture quotations, unless otherwise noted, are taken from the Holy Bible, New International Version®, NIV®. Copyright © 1973, 1978, 1984, 2011 by Biblica, Inc.® Used by permission. All rights reserved worldwide.

Scripture quotations marked ESV are taken from the ESV® Bible (The Holy Bible, English Standard Version®). Copyright © 2001 by Crossway, a publishing ministry of Good News Publishers. Used by permission. All rights reserved.

Any internet addresses (websites, blogs, etc.) and telephone numbers in this study guide are offered as a resource. They are not intended in any way to be or imply an endorsement by HarperChristian Resources, nor does HarperChristian Resources vouch for the content of these sites and numbers for the life of this study guide.

All rights reserved. No portion of this book may be reproduced, stored in a retrieval system, or transmitted in any form or by any means—electronic, mechanical, photocopy, recording, scanning, or other—except for brief quotations in critical reviews or articles, without the prior written permission of the publisher.

HarperChristian Resources titles may be purchased in bulk for church, business, fundraising, or ministry use. For information, please e-mail ResourceSpecialist@ChurchSource.com.

First Printing April 2025 / Printed in the United States of America

CONTENTS

A Note from Gary v

How to Use This Guide vii

SESSION 1: GOD'S PURPOSE FOR MARRIAGE

Group Session 1

Personal (or Couple) Study 7

    Study 1: Holiness Leads to Happiness 8

    Study 2: Mirrors and Marriage 11

    Study 3: Putting First Things First 14

    Catch Up and Read Ahead 17

SESSION 2: THE REFINING POWER OF MARRIAGE

Group Session 19

Personal (or Couple) Study 25

    Study 1: Hang in There 26

    Study 2: Examine Expectations 29

    Study 3: Build Endurance 32

    Catch Up and Read Ahead 35

SESSION 3: THE GOD-CENTERED SPOUSE

Group Session 37

Personal (or Couple) Study 43

    Study 1: God as Your Heavenly Father 44

    Study 2: God as Your Spouse's Heavenly Father 47

    Study 3: God-Centered or Spouse-Centered? 50

    Catch Up and Read Ahead 55

SESSION 4: MARRIAGE: THE LOVE LABORATORY

Group Session 57

Personal (or Couple) Study 63

    Study 1: God's Design of Differences 64

    Study 2: Christianity = Love 67

    Study 3: The Perfect Laboratory for Love 70

    Catch Up and Read Ahead 73

SESSION 5: SEXUAL SAINTS

Group Session 75
Personal (or Couple) Study 81

    Study 1: Go to the Source 82
    Study 2: Pleasure for All 85
    Study 3: Sacred Sexuality 88
    Catch Up and Read Ahead 91

SESSION 6: SACRED HISTORY

Group Session 93
Personal (or Couple) Study 99

    Study 1: The Journey from *Me* to *We* 100
    Study 2: The Essential Place of Perseverance 103
    Study 3: The Hardest Season 106
    Wrap It Up 109

Leader's Guide 111
About the Author and Writers 115

A NOTE FROM GARY

Lisa and I have been married for more than forty years—and we still really like each other. Our love has grown as we have laughed, played, prayed, and celebrated the joys of marriage for about two-thirds of our lives. Our love has also matured as we have struggled, wept, fought, and pressed through times of unspeakable pain and loss. Every step of the way God has surrounded us with his grace and given us strength to persevere even when we felt uncertain about exactly how to press forward.

We have raised three children and are now grandparents. When the book, *Sacred Marriage*, was first released, we were in a season of marriage with a home filled with kids and constant activities. Now we are empty nesters who live in the middle of the country, and we look for opportunities to spend time with our children who are scattered in two different states from coast to coast.

Through the years and seasons of marriage, we have discovered that so many of the lessons found in *Sacred Marriage* speak truth every step of the journey. We also know that the unchanging message of God's Word can be expressed in fresh ways for each generation. With this in mind, you hold in your hands an updated study guide based on the book, *Sacred Marriage*. Many of the major themes have stayed the same, but the introductions, video teaching, questions, and activities have been updated to speak with clarity to a new generation of learners and to those who have already been familiar with these resources.

May the God who made you and who delights every time that two become one fill your hearts, home, and marriage with his presence.

— GARY THOMAS

HOW TO USE THIS GUIDE

What if marriage was designed by God to make us holy more than to make us happy? This was the question addressed in *Sacred Marriage* when it was released two and a half decades ago. It is a question that has struck a chord in the hearts of many people through the years. Now, to be clear, happiness is a great blessing, and a Jesus-centered marriage is the pathway to the happiest marriage. But the deeper question is . . . *Did God invent marriage for more than our personal pleasure and happiness?* The answer is a resounding *yes!*

The purpose of this study is to help married couples (and couples considering marriage) get a biblical and God-honoring vision of marriage. From moments of prayer as a couple to the richest places of physical intimacy, God wants to use marriage to transform our hearts, motives, dreams, and every part of who we are to be more like our Savior. This study guide is designed to work in partnership with the book *Sacred Marriage* and the video content to take you on a journey of growth in one of the most important relationships in your life, marriage.

Before you begin, know that there are a few ways you can go through this material. You can experience this study with others in a group (such as a Bible study, Sunday school class, or other gathering), or you can go through the content on your own. Either way, the videos are available to view at any time by following the instructions provided in this study guide.

GROUP STUDY

Each of the sessions in this study is divided into two parts: (1) a group study section, and (2) a personal study section. The group study section provides a basic framework for opening your time together, getting the most out of the video content, and discussing the key ideas presented in the teaching. Each session includes the following:

- **Welcome:** A short opening note about the topic of the session for you to read on your own before you meet as a group.
- **Connect:** A few icebreaker questions to get you and your group members thinking about the topic and interacting with each other.

- **Watch:** An outline of the key points covered in each video teaching along with space for you to take notes as you watch each session.
- **Discuss:** Questions to help you and your group reflect on the teaching material presented and apply it to your lives.
- **Respond:** A short personal exercise to help reinforce the key ideas.
- **Pray:** A place for you to record prayer requests and praises for the week.

If you are doing this study in a group, make sure you have your own copy of the study guide so you can write down your thoughts, responses, and reflections in the space provided—and so you have access to the videos via streaming. You will also want to have a copy of the *Sacred Marriage* book, as reading it alongside this guide will provide you with deeper insights. (See the notes at the beginning of each group session and personal/couple study section on which chapters of the book you might want to review before the next group session.)

Finally, keep these points in mind:

- **Facilitation:** If you are doing this study in a group, you will want to appoint some-one to serve as a facilitator. This person will be responsible for starting the video and keeping track of time during discussions and activities. If *you* have been cho-sen for this role, there are some resources in the back of this guide that can help you lead your group through the study.

- **Faithfulness:** Your group is a place where tremendous growth can happen as you reflect on the Bible, ask questions, and learn what God is doing in other people's lives. For this reason, be fully committed and attend each session so you can build trust and rapport with the other members.

- **Friendship:** The goal of any small group is to serve as a place where people can share, learn about God, and build friendships. So seek to make your group a wel-coming place. Be honest about your thoughts and feelings, but also listen carefully to everyone else's thoughts, feelings, and opinions. Keep anything personal that your group members share in confidence so that you can create a community where people can heal, be challenged, and grow spiritually.

If you are going through this study on your own, read the opening Welcome section and reflect on the questions in the Connect section. Watch the video and use the outline provided to help you take notes. Finally, personalize the questions and exercises in the Discuss and Respond sections. Close by recording any requests you want to pray about during the week.

PERSONAL (OR COUPLE) STUDY

This section is for you to work through on your own *or* you and your spouse to work through together during the week. Each exercise will help you explore ideas presented during the group time and delve into passages that will help you apply those principles to your life. (You will also find excerpts from the video teaching interspersed throughout this section in gray shaded boxes.) Go at your own pace, doing a little each day, or tackle the material all at once. Remember to spend a few moments in silence to listen to what God might be saying to you.

If you are doing this study as part of a group, and you (or you and your spouse) are unable to finish these studies for the week, you both should still attend the group time. Be assured you are still wanted and welcome even if you don't have your "homework" done. The group studies and personal studies are intended to help you hear what God wants you to hear and how to apply what he is saying to your life. So . . . as you go through this study, be listening for him to open your eyes to a fresh new understanding of marriage that reflects the heart of God, the Word of God, and the dreams that God has for your marriage.

WEEK 1

BEFORE GROUP MEETING	Review chapters 1–3 in *Sacred Marriage* Read the Welcome section (page 2)
GROUP MEETING	Discuss the Connect questions Watch the video teaching for session 1 Discuss the questions that follow as a group Do the closing exercise and pray (pages 2–6)
STUDY 1	Complete the personal (or couple) study (pages 8–10)
STUDY 2	Complete the personal (or couple) study (pages 11–13)
STUDY 3	Complete the personal (or couple) study (pages 14–16)
CATCH UP & READ AHEAD (BEFORE WEEK 2 GROUP MEETING)	Read chapters 5–7 in *Sacred Marriage* Complete any unfinished personal studies (page 17)

SESSION ONE

GOD'S PURPOSE FOR MARRIAGE

Marriage is a divinely designed relationship that can make us more like Jesus and grow us in holiness with each passing year. A healthy marriage can bring joy and lead to happiness, but God offers much more.

WELCOME | READ ON YOUR OWN

God does not waste any life experience. Each day offers opportunities for growth, joy, meaning, sacrifice, and more. God loves to see his children grow to be more like Jesus and reflect our Savior's love and presence in this world. Our Maker accomplishes his will in us through things such as meaningful labor, parenting, family relationships, friendships, church life, neighbors, difficult people, hobbies, and almost everything we experience.

But among our life experiences, there is one that seems to dig the deepest into our soul and shape our character more than any other: *marriage*! The US Census Bureau still says approximately 90 percent of Americans will get married at some point in their lives. Some see the marriage relationship as primarily a fusion of body and soul that leads to happiness and pleasure. For some, marriage is a responsibility or a duty that must be endured. There are people whose primary framework for marriage is self-satisfaction and enjoyment. But God's design for marriage is richer and more profound than any of these outlooks.

Marriage has a God-ordained and sacred purpose. The intimacy and closeness of a man and woman in the covenant of marriage is the perfect setting for God to grow them into the image of Jesus and develop personal holiness. If we approach marriage with a heavenly perspective, it can be one of life's most glorious pursuits. On the other hand, when we see marriage as the guarantee of personal happiness, unending pleasure, and having a partner to meet our needs, it can quickly deteriorate into frustration and pain.

Building a healthy marriage is one of the greatest challenges we will face. Yet when we listen to God's wisdom and walk where the Holy Spirit leads, it can be a life-transforming adventure that shapes our soul and connects us deeply to our spouse and God's heart.

CONNECT | 10 MINUTES

If you or any of your group members don't know each other, take a few minutes to introduce yourselves. Then discuss one or both of the following questions:

- Why did you decide to join this study? What do you hope to learn?

  — or —

- Share one way that being married has stretched you, grown you, and made you more like the Savior who died on the cross to win your salvation.

Session One: God's Purpose for Marriage

WATCH | 25 MINUTES

Watch the video for this session, which you can access by playing the DVD or through streaming (see the instructions provided with this guide). Below is an outline of the key points covered during the teaching. Record any key concepts that stand out to you.

OUTLINE

I. There is something about a wedding.
  A. What if God wants to give us more than just one big happy day?
  B. What if God desires to make us holy more than happy?
  C. Wise words from John Wesley.
  D. Holiness is the pathway to the happiest of marriages.
  E. Gary and Lisa's "ice tray" moment . . . what is yours?
II. How marriage shows you deeper parts of yourself.
  A. Some of us don't like mirrors.
  B. The perspective of Frances de Sales.
  C. You can't have a healthy marriage without a spiritually healthy you.
  D. How personal sin impacts a marriage.
III. Seeking God first transforms a marriage (Matthew 6:33).
  A. Understanding holiness.
  B. Holiness is becoming whole or spiritually healthy (2 Corinthians 7:1).
  C. A one-time decision that leads to an all-the-time pursuit.
  D. Story of Rhett and Kristy.
IV. What if God's agenda is very different than ours?
  A. Marriage as a spiritual gymnasium.
  B. Using our marriage to destroy sin instead of letting sin destroy our marriage.
  C. The problem of wrong expectations.
  D. Compare your righteousness not to your spouse but to your Savior
V. Marriage is not about being fulfilled, emotionally satisfied, or romantically fulfilled.
  A. It is a way to become more like Jesus.
  B. When we die to false expectations, we can find real joy in marriage.
  C. Too many people think they need a new partner when they actually need is a new perspective.
  D. Being married for the glory of God gives great hope for the future.

NOTES

Session One: God's Purpose for Marriage

DISCUSS | 35 MINUTES

Discuss what you just watched by answering the following questions.

1. Gary shared about his ice tray encounter and facing family history differences between himself and Lisa early in their marriage. Tell about an "ice tray" moment you have faced in your marriage. Why does it seem so silly when you look back now?

2. Ask someone to read Matthew 6:33, Galatians 5:22–23, and Ephesians 5:22–23. How can seeking God's kingdom first (his will in all things) grow us in holiness and fortify our marriage relationship? What is one fruit of the Spirit that you need to grow in your life? How can others encourage you in this part of your spiritual life?

3. Ask someone to read 2 Corinthians 7:1. What are some of the things that contaminate our body and spirit that negatively impact our marriage? What are ways we can avoid these and orient our lives toward holiness and the things that please God?

4. How is it true that you can't have a spiritually healthy marriage if there isn't a spiritually healthy *you*? What can you do at this point in your life to more earnestly pursue spiritual health and grow your marriage accordingly?

5. Sometimes, when marriage is hard, we think the solution is to find a new partner. A better outlook is to realize we need a new *perception*. In light of what you have learned in this session and in being married, what fresh perceptions about marriage can help you align with God's plan for this mysterious and glorious relationship?

RESPOND | 10 MINUTES

Identify one way your patterns, attitude, or behavior might be irritating to your spouse. Make a commitment to do your best to change this behavior as a sign of love for your spouse. (For instance, if your spouse loves a full ice tray and you don't normally fill it up, make a commitment to fill it every time you take ice.) Now read this passage:

> Love is patient, love is kind. It does not envy, it does not boast, it is not proud. It does not dishonor others, it is not self-seeking, it is not easily angered, it keeps no record of wrongs.
>
> 1 CORINTHIANS 13:4–5

Think about an "ice tray" irritation you deal with. Is the problem primarily that you *let* it annoy you? How can you navigate it as a couple?

How can you begin to use "ice tray" moments to reveal your heart and attitudes? How does an earnest desire to grow in holiness change the way you view such moments?

PRAY | 10 MINUTES

Close by thanking God for the gift your spouse is to you, including your spouse's role as your brother or sister in Christ. Ask him to grow your personal holiness and make you more like Jesus so you will discover new expressions of happiness in your marriage. Invite the Holy Spirit to guide and grow you through the "ice tray" moments you experience. Pray for discipline to devote more time in the "gym" of spiritual growth so it will lead to greater health and happiness in your marriage.

SESSION **ONE**

PERSONAL (OR COUPLE) STUDY

Use these studies to go deeper into the topics discussed during your group time. It is ideal to do these studies as a couple, but some may want to do them on their own. The most important thing is that you spend time digging in deeper before your next group gathering. As you work through these exercises, be sure to write down your responses to the questions. (If you are engaging in this study as part of a group, you will be given a few minutes to share your insights at the start of the next session.) If you are reading *Sacred Marriage* alongside this study, you may want to first review chapters 1–3 of the book.

STUDY 1

HOLINESS LEADS TO HAPPINESS

Holiness is a great theme for worship songs and old hymns. We can lift our voices and sing, "Holy, holy, holy, Lord God Almighty, God in three persons, blessed Trinity." Every word is true. We mean it when we sing it. We might even get a little misty-eyed and nostalgic as a whole church lifts up these words in unison with voices and hearts joined together.

Those who follow Jesus and who take the Bible seriously know that God is perfectly holy. The problem is that we often fail to see how holiness fits into our lives. Theologically, we might know that through faith in Jesus, we will be made holy one day, but few of us wake up, look in the mirror, and say, "You are looking pretty holy today." If anything, we live with an awareness that holiness evades us much of the time.

As for holiness in our marriage, this is likely a new thought for most people. With all the demands and expectations set on husbands and wives, the idea of paying close attention to our personal holiness does not come up on the radar of most of our marriages.

The truth is that few things are more important for a healthy, thriving, happy marriage than becoming more like Jesus. Turning from worldly and personal sin and seeking the will of God is a powerful gift to a marriage relationship. Marital thriving is closely connected to our pursuit of holiness. Pause right now and ask the perfectly holy God of eternity to open your eyes, heart, and life to a new understanding of his will, Word, and ways as you seek holiness in your life, heart, and home.

1. When you think of holiness, what ideas, pictures, and practices come to your mind? (Use the space provided to write words, draw images, or list spiritual practices.)

Session One: God's Purpose for Marriage

2. Read Colossians 3:8–9, 12–14. How can the negative things that Paul tells us to "put off" and the positive virtues that Paul tells us to "put on" affect the health and happiness of a marriage in negative ways?

When I say that God designed marriage to make us holy even more than to make us happy, notice I didn't say instead of happy. I love the words of the great evangelist John Wesley, who said, "I've never met anyone who is truly happy, who is not pursuing holiness." If somebody doesn't have his or her anger under control, that person ends up pushing people away. They're not happy. Addicts have moments of pleasure but far more moments of misery. I would say holiness preserves happiness. It doesn't undercut it. So when I say that God designed marriage to make us holy even more than to make us happy, we could say that holiness is the pathway to the happiest marriages.

3. If husbands and wives are growing in holiness (they are becoming whole in Jesus) and their attitudes and actions are aligning with God's will in growing measure, how could this affect their marriage for the better?

4. Read Hebrews 12:14–15. How does holiness draw us closer to God? How does a lack of holiness in our life drive us away from God?

Sacred Marriage Bible Study

None of us can change our spouse, but all of us, with the power of the Holy Spirit, can change our marriage by pursuing holiness out of reverence for God. Marriage isn't primarily about being fulfilled, emotionally satisfied, or romantically charged. In the heart of God, marriage is a powerful way for each of us to become more like Jesus and to fulfill God's call for us to seek his kingdom first. A holier you leads to a healthier you, which leads to a happier you, which leads to a happier marriage. We will all face the normal struggles of becoming more like Jesus, but here's the great hope: God designed marriage to make us holy even more than to make us happy. And, when we grow in holiness, happiness seems to blossom in our homes and marriages.

5. What is one specific action you are going to take to do your part to grow in holiness? How can your spouse pray as you take this step in spiritual growth?

An area where I need to grow in holiness:

What is keeping me from moving forward in this area of my life:

My actions:

My prayers:

STUDY 2

MIRRORS AND MARRIAGE

Mike had always had a bit of a temper. As a kid, Dad and Mom mostly laughed it off and called him passionate. Through the years, his coaches fanned the flames when he got fiery because it made him play harder. His friends thought it was kind of funny, and they would do all they could to push Mike's buttons until he "lost it."

Amanda seemed to have a gift. She could see people's faults and was comfortable pointing them out. She was not intentionally malicious. But she did have a way of frequently bringing up people's mistakes. Most of her friends and family members grew so used to it that they gave Amanda a pass when she was being "a little negative."

All of us have our faults and weaknesses. God wants to refine us and make us better people, but many of our places of brokenness and sin can go unnoticed or unchecked. The holy and God-ordained relationship of marriage provides a mirror to show us our sins with clarity.

When God brought Mike and Amanda together, a transformation process started. Amanda was quick to point out Mike's fiery nature. Mike's response was to get even more intense. Rather than thanking her for honest perspective, he pointed out that she was critical and negative . . . "all the time!"

Over the coming years, God used Mike and Amanda like mirrors to show each other places of needed growth. With time, prayer, lots of conversation, and humility in each of their hearts, God used their marriage to make both Mike and Amanda more like Jesus. Mike was still intense and had to watch his temper, but he was learning to tone it down and even grow in gentleness. Amanda still saw negative things intuitively, but she was learning that it was not her role to tell everyone where they were in the wrong.

Marriage is a mirror that God uses to help us become more like Jesus.

○ Sacred Marriage Bible Study

1. Think about one way God has used your spouse to help you see an area where you needed to grow. Think also about how God has changed your life for the better and made you more like Jesus because of your spouse. Now answer the questions below.

> Write an area of growth God has used your spouse to accelerate in your life:

> Now write a note of thanks to God and your spouse for this gift of partnership in spiritual growth and read it to your spouse:

2. Read Psalm 139:1–6, 23–24. What do you learn about how God sees you and knows everything about you? How does God use your spouse in the process of searching you and helping you see areas of needed growth?

Marriage is like a giant mirror that reveals what people are really like—and some people don't like mirrors that much. It makes them want to run from what they're seeing. They might be ashamed of what they did and said in their marriage. So they are unwilling to look into that mirror of their spouse and believe what they see. Instead, they are quick to blame things on the person they married. Sadly, they get into their second or third marriage before they realize the same issues arise over and over because they brought them along. This is why we need to look honestly into the marriage mirror and deal with what we see.

Session One: God's Purpose for Marriage

3. Why is it often hard when God uses our spouses as a magnifying glass to help us see an area of needed growth that we have failed to notice? Why do we need to be very humble in these moments?

4. Read 2 Corinthians 7:1. We are called to be purified from everything (big and small, inside and outside). What is an area in which God has been purifying you or one you know he wants to grow you in holiness? How can your spouse pray with you and encourage you in this area?

Write down three ways your spouse can be praying for you in this specific area, and share these to help direct his or her intercession for you.

1. _____
2. _____
3. _____

It is easy to justify our faults and say, "I don't think I'm that bad." But Paul doesn't say to purify ourselves from only the worst things. He says we should purify ourselves from *everything* that contaminates body and spirit. Not just the gross scandalous sins, but also the attitudinal ones. In the original Greek, this is in the present tense. It's an ongoing process. We will never be perfect, but out of reverence for all that God has given us—his forgiveness, the power of the Holy Spirit, the direction of his word—we are to make the pursuit of holiness our earnest aim. In other words, Christianity is a decision that unleashes an all-the-time pursuit.

5. What is an area of spiritual growth that you have seen increasing in the life of your spouse? (Encourage and celebrate this area of growth.)

STUDY 3

PUTTING FIRST THINGS FIRST

In the classic movie *The Sound of Music*, there is a scene where the Von Trapp children are learning to sing. Up to this point, music was not allowed in their home or lives. They are taught a song titled "Do-Re-Mi." Their new nanny explains to the children (in song) that there are fundamentals for everything in life. When you read, you begin with A-B-C. When you sing, you begin with Do-Re-Mi. What follows is a music lesson in the beautiful mountains of Austria.

The point is obvious: *Fundamentals lead to learning and growth*. Math teachers begin with 1-2-3. Few of them sing these words, and even fewer math teachers dance around the room as they educate the children in these mathematical basics, but they know their students can't move on to the complex stuff until they nail down the fundamentals. Once the kids know the numbers and basic counting, then addition, subtraction, and even multiplication and division all make more sense. You get the picture.

Jesus, likewise, began with the foundations of spiritual growth. He said, "But seek first the kingdom of God and his righteousness, and all these things will be added to you" (Matthew 6:33 ESV). Our Savior knew that if we were not seeking God's will and ways, nothing else in life would really make sense.

This lesson applies beautifully to marriage. The best gift you can give your spouse is a vibrant and growing spiritual life. Love Jesus. Grow in his Word. Seek his face. Increase in holiness. Care about his kingdom more than you care about your own. Everything else will follow. On the other hand, if you miss these basics, nothing else in marriage will fully make sense.

A-B-C, 1-2-3, Do-Re-Mi, "Seek first the kingdom of God." The fundamentals.

Session One: God's Purpose for Marriage

1. Why is it necessary to get fundamentals right before we move to the more complex things in life? What problems might we face if we fail to start with the basics?

Write down one area of interest in your life (from baking to law to martial arts to dance . . . anything):

Write down three basics or fundamentals that are needed to do this well:

1. _____

2. _____

3. _____

2. Read Matthew 6:28–34. What is the heartbeat of what Jesus is saying in this passage? Why do you think seeking first God's kingdom and what he wants is the best starting place for a healthy marriage?

You can't have a healthy marriage if there isn't a spiritually healthy *you*. Anger isn't a marriage issue. It's a personal issue that can be devastating to a marriage. Arrogance, being full of yourself, having a critical spirit, laziness . . . these are personal issues that undercut marital health and happiness. If you want to have a better marriage, engage in what Jesus calls everyone to do: "Seek first the kingdom of God and his righteousness" (Matthew 6:33 ESV). If we are seeking first his righteousness, we are dying to the character traits that destroy most relationships.

○ Sacred Marriage Bible Study

3. We are all tempted to seek other things first. Make a list of five things you can be tempted to seek first rather than the kingdom of God and his righteousness. (For example: looking younger than you are instead of growing in character, earning more money and saving a certain amount for retirement, or getting a bigger house.)

1. _____
2. _____
3. _____
4. _____
5. _____

Share this list with your spouse and ask for prayer and encouragement as you learn to put these things second, third, or further down the list in your life.

4. What is one spiritual practice that will help you grow in faith and keep Jesus and his kingdom on the front burner of your heart and life? How can you increase your engagement in this practice?

We all know it takes commitment, work, and discipline to get into physical shape. So why do we think it's any different for us to stay in spiritual shape? We work, sweat, and push our bodies because we know the results will be worth it. We want to be stronger, faster, healthier, and live longer. So what if we looked at marriage as a spiritual gymnasium? Why do we keep forgiving? Why do we ask for forgiveness? Why do we learn to serve? Why do we seek to walk in humility? Because our marriage is helping us become more like Jesus.

5. Consistent workouts demand a plan, time, place, and measurable goals. When it comes to your spiritual health, describe the details of your plan. (If you don't have one, that might be a clue to your struggles. Make a plan and share with your spouse.)

CATCH UP AND READ AHEAD

Take some time today to reflect on everything that you have learned this week. If you have been doing this study section on your own, connect with your spouse and discuss some of these key insights. Use any of the following prompts to help guide this time.

- What did you like best from the content in this session, including both the group study and personal study? Why?
- What are some of the unrealistic, idealistic, and eventually dangerous expectations we can place on our spouse (or the concept of marriage), and why is it helpful to identify these and name them for what they are?
- What are some examples of what it might look like as a couple to seek God's will and ways (to seek his kingdom) in your marriage relationship in the flow of normal life? How can you take a step forward in actively doing one of these things as a couple in the coming weeks?
- Tell about a time when you were really connected with Jesus and were doing your best to seek the will and ways of the Savior, including prioritizing his kingdom (his authority and rule) over your own. How did your consistent seeking of Jesus affect your marriage relationship?
- What do you feel most excited to explore in the sessions ahead? Why?

Use this time to go back and complete any of the study and reflection questions from previous days that you weren't able to finish. Make a note below of any revelations you've had and reflect on any growth or personal insights you've gained.

You may wish to review chapters 5–7 in *Sacred Marriage* before the next gathering. Make note below of anything in those chapters that stands out to you or encourages you.

WEEK 2

BEFORE GROUP MEETING	Review chapters 5–7 in *Sacred Marriage* Read the Welcome section (page 20)
GROUP MEETING	Discuss the Connect questions Watch the video teaching for session 2 Discuss the questions that follow as a group Do the closing exercise and pray (pages 20–24)
STUDY 1	Complete the personal (or couple) study (pages 26–28)
STUDY 2	Complete the personal (or couple) study (pages 29–31)
STUDY 3	Complete the personal (or couple) study (pages 32–34)
CATCH UP & READ AHEAD (BEFORE WEEK 3 GROUP MEETING)	Review chapter 4 in *Sacred Marriage* Complete any unfinished personal studies (page 35)

SESSION TWO

THE REFINING POWER OF MARRIAGE

Every human being is imperfect and stumbles along the way. When two imperfect people are brought together by a perfect God, challenges are guaranteed. If we hang in there and devote ourselves to building a strong marriage, God will do more in us (individually and as a couple) than we could have ever dreamed.

WELCOME | READ ON YOUR OWN

If you want to purify gold, it takes heat. Depending on the purity of the gold, the refining process happens between 1,832 and 2,192 degrees Fahrenheit. Water boils at 212 degrees Fahrenheit. The refining heat for gold is close to *ten times* hotter.

If you want a beautiful diamond, you need pressure over time. It takes around 825,000 pounds per square inch over massive amounts of time to create the raw materials needed for a diamond. Then you need a gifted lapidary (gem cutter) with the right tools to carefully shape the diamond into something stunning. If you want to become an elite athlete, it takes practice. Professional marathoners can be on the road 90 to 140 miles a week as part of their training. Top Olympic swimmers can be in the pool 25 to 30 hours a week. This does not include weight training, food preparation, and recovery exercises.

If you want to become a mature Christian and grow deep in faith, marriage can be one of God's best routes to get you there. Why? Well, like refining gold, marriage brings heat. Like forming a diamond, marriage produces pressure. Like athletic training, marriage demands time, practice, devotion, and perseverance.

Simply put, there is a divinely inspired refining power to marriage. If you commit yourself to build a lasting, healthy, loving, Jesus-led marriage, every part of your life will be tested and transformed. God will use the adventure of marriage to shape you into more than you would ever have been if you had walked through life alone. But it won't be easy!

CONNECT | 10 MINUTES

If you or any of your group members don't know each other, take a few minutes to introduce yourselves. Then discuss one or both of the following questions:

- What is something that spoke to you in last week's personal study that you would like to share with the group?

— *or* —

- Think of something you tried to do but found it was too hard to keep pursuing. What regrets do you have for not pushing through the challenge and learning how to do that particular thing?

Session Two: The Refining Power of Marriage

WATCH | 25 MINUTES

Now watch the video for this session. Below is an outline of the key points covered during the teaching. Record any key concepts that stand out to you.

OUTLINE

I. Gary got a lyre . . . some things are harder than you think.
   A. Building a beautiful marriage is harder than we think.
   B. We all stumble in many ways (James 3:2).
   C. No one is righteous, not you or your spouse (Romans 3:10).
   D. When marriage gets tough, don't freak out!
II. Your expectations of marriage will have a huge impact on your marriage.
   A. *What if I married the wrong person?*
   B. A truck story.
   C. Idealism about marriage can lead to frustration.
III. Healthy marriages demand endurance.
   A. Endure hardship (2 Timothy 4:5).
   B. Life is difficult so marriage will be difficult.
   C. Difficulty draws us to Jesus.
   D. Jesus told us we will have trouble in this world (John 16:33).

NOTES

NOTES

Session Two: The Refining Power of Marriage

DISCUSS | 35 MINUTES

Discuss what you just watched by answering the following questions.

1. Read James 3:2 and Romans 3:10–12. Why is it absolutely essential that you recognize that everyone (including you and your spouse) stumbles in many ways? What dangers are you sure to encounter in your marriage relationship if you don't embrace this truth and live with a clear awareness of the sinful nature of every human being?

2. If you enter marriage with unhealthy and unbiblical expectations, you will end up surprised every time something goes wrong. What were some of the wrong expectations you brought into marriage (or maybe still have)? How can these be corrected?

3. Ask someone to read aloud 2 Timothy 4:5. Paul challenges Timothy to keep his head no matter what he faces, hang in there during the hard times, and fulfill the work God called him to do. How can each of these three charges be applied to marriage?

4. When you think of the three lessons and exhortations from Paul, which of these do you need to tend to in your marriage? How might this be a blessing to your spouse?

5. When you look on the horizon of your married life (including family, work, faith, finances, and all marriage entails), what is a challenge you see coming your way? How can others pray for your marriage and encourage you as you press into the future?

RESPOND | 10 MINUTES

One of the reasons it makes sense to see the Bible as a divine book and not the creation of people is that it is so honest about our frailties, rebellion, and sin. The Bible is explicit in its portrayal of people. As the following passage relates, from the beginning of time to today, human beings stumble and fall on a shockingly frequent basis. This should concern and comfort us. The concern is that we are human and still enticed to sin, and sin always has consequences. The comfort comes from knowing we are not alone in our struggle.

> The LORD saw how great the wickedness of the human race had become on the earth, and that every inclination of the thoughts of the human heart was only evil all the time. The LORD regretted that he had made human beings on the earth, and his heart was deeply troubled. . . . Now the earth was corrupt in God's sight and was full of violence. God saw how corrupt the earth had become, for all the people on earth had corrupted their ways.
>
> GENESIS 6:5–6, 11–12

How does the picture of people in Genesis connect with what James says about all people stumbling in many ways?

Why is it so important for you to understand the battle with sin and the way all people fall short of God's intentions and dreams for them?

PRAY | 10 MINUTES

Lift up prayers of thanks to God that he sees your imperfections and still loves you. Pray you will do the same for others. Ask for grace for yourself and your spouse when you fall short and make mistakes. Give God thanks for growing your love for him and for each other during the hard times you have faced as a couple. Ask the Holy Spirit to help you resist the temptation to run from each other when brokenness is present.

SESSION TWO

PERSONAL (OR COUPLE) STUDY

In the first session, we focused on how God designed marriage to make us both holy and happy. Most of the time we focus on the happiness side of the equation. In this session, our attention shifted to the important reality that marriage is difficult because life has challenges. To move toward a healthy, holy, and happy marriage, we need to acknowledge challenges, examine our expectations, and develop endurance. Keep this in mind as you work through these exercises. Write down your responses to the questions, as you will be given a few minutes to share your insights at the start of the next session if you are doing this study with others. If you are reading *Sacred Marriage* alongside this study, you may want to first review chapters 5–7 in the book.

STUDY 1

HANG IN THERE

Gardening is one of the most popular hobbies. People love to plant seeds, water, weed, water more, clear out bugs, water more, weed more . . . you get the picture. Gardening demands patience, hard work, and relentless attention. When pests attack, you fight them off. When the sun scorches, you protect your garden. If there is a cold snap, you cover up vulnerable plants.

You rarely hear a gardener complain that they have to water regularly. It is understood that this is part of the process. Fruit and vegetable gardeners know they will have an ongoing battle with bugs, bunnies, and birds, so they prepare. If gardeners gave up on their plants and trees when they discovered this hobby would take work, there would be no gardeners.

But there *are* tons of gardens out there. Most gardeners don't give up. They do the work. They stick with it. And they get the fruit of their labors when they serve fresh vegetables from their garden. They delight in the lovely bouquet made with their freshly cut flowers. They smile with satisfaction when they bite into a plump strawberry they just picked.

If only couples went into marriage with the same kind of awareness and anticipation of the upcoming difficulties as gardeners have when they plant their seeds. If married couples anticipated lots of watering, weeding, and battles with little pests and critters, they would be far less discouraged. Most marriages would be healthier and happier if the husband and wife both expected challenges, welcomed difficulties, and committed to the daily work it takes to care for their beautiful and God-ordained marriage garden.

Marriage is difficult, but it is worth all the hard work. Get ready to water with love, pick relational weeds with patience, and fight off the regular attacks that will come. In the end, there will be a wonderful harvest, so hang in there.

1. Read James 3:2 and Romans 3:10–12. What are some ways married people stumble? Why is it important not to give up on your spouse when stumbling occurs?

Session Two: The Refining Power of Marriage

2. What are some comparisons you can think of between gardening and marriage?

Marriage   **Gardening**

_____ is like _____

_____ is like _____

_____ is like _____

_____ is like _____

Why do you think so many people give up on marriage rather than facing the difficulties as part of the deal?

You can have a beautiful marriage, but it's going to be difficult to get there. You will have to learn how to forgive and ask for forgiveness. The path might prove to be difficult, and you can't just give up when the road gets hard. But when difficulties hit, don't assume there's something wrong with marriage. You need to be willing to travel *through* the difficulty it takes to get to the beautiful music behind marriage.

3. Finish the following statements with a few practical ideas.

> If I am going to have a healthy marriage, I should start to . . .

○ Sacred Marriage Bible Study

> If I am going to have a healthy marriage, I should stop . . .

4. Think about a time of intense challenge that you and your spouse walked through together. Write down some of the ways this journey has deepened your faith, strengthened your marriage, or brought you closer together.

I've met many people who seem shocked when their marriage proves to be difficult. They assume they must have chosen the wrong person. When someone says, "I'm in a difficult marriage," I say to myself, *That's a redundant statement.* If marriage is one person who stumbles in many ways, marrying another person who stumbles in many ways—then having sex and creating little people who stumble in many ways—why would we think it is going to be easy?

5. What helps you show patience and kindness with your spouse during difficult times? How does this process strengthen your marriage and help you endure?

STUDY 2

EXAMINE EXPECTATIONS

"You have to try the newest Mexican restaurant in town. It is amazing! They make the best guacamole in the world. Everything is fresh and delicious. It will blow your mind."

"I am going to send you a YouTube link for my favorite comedian. It is so funny you will laugh until it hurts. It is brilliant and maybe the best comedy I have ever seen."

"I really want to take you to see the new sequel to one of my favorite movies. I'll pay your way and buy popcorn. I've already watched it twice and it will change your life!"

What do these three short scenarios have in common? They are setting someone up for disappointment. Have you ever had a person oversell something and promise a life-changing, side-splitting, taste-bud-transforming experience? Most of the time, the hype predisposes us to expect more than can be delivered.

When it comes to marriage, our culture can misrepresent what this union is about. When eyes lock in a tender moment of a romantic comedy and he looks at her and says, "You complete me," false expectations are instilled in the heart of every viewer. When princess films present the fairy-tale happily ever after, it is not fair. When engaged couples look forward to mind-blowing intimacy every time they go into the bedroom, because Hollywood presents unrealistic storylines, disappointment is on the horizon.

When a couple anticipates no conflict but only peaceful and smooth sailing all the days of their voyage together, it just might end up being a short trip. What we need is realistic and biblical expectations!

1. What are some false expectations people have going into marriage? What was one of your expectations that was not reflective of real life when it comes to marriage?

Sacred Marriage Bible Study

2. Read 1 John 1:5–7. John is clear that we can walk in darkness and barely realize it is happening. What are some of the things in your world (and in your life) that can cause you to walk in darkness? How can this effect your married life?

> If we enter marriage with idealistic notions that everything will be easy if we just pick the right person, we are going to be disappointed. Our expectations of what we think marriage should be is one of the biggest influencers of how content we will be in our marriage. When a couple measures their marriage by what they think it should be, not how God designed it to be, it leads to shell-shocked newlyweds. They think they married the wrong person because things have turned out more difficult than they imagined.

3. After spending some time on this topic of false expectations in marriage, what is one expectation you are still living with that needs to be set aside for the truth? What is a more biblical and truthful way to look at this and have proper expectations?

Session Two: The Refining Power of Marriage

4. Read 1 John 1:8–10. This passage uncovers the prevalence of having a wrong view of who we are and how we behave. Why is an accurate view of our own battle with sin needed if we are going to live with godly expectations in marriage?

5. What is one way you can show grace and kindness to your spouse even when he or she stumbles? How can you show this same grace to yourself?

For some people, their preconceived view of marriage is sacrosanct. They won't question it. Instead, they question their spousal choice. They have a hard time recognizing that if they had married someone else, they would be dealing with another list of ways people stumble. If we believe Scripture, we will expect stumbling in our lives and the lives of our spouses. This does not excuse bad behavior, it just sets us up with the right expectations. There will be difficult times, but God can use those difficult times for very good things. As a matter of fact, some of the best things in life are difficult!

STUDY 3

BUILD ENDURANCE

Designed, intentional, strategic obsolescence. It is all around us. Whatever phone you carry around in your pocket or purse will likely be out of date way before it stops working. The designers know they can charge $1,000 or even more for many of these devices.

Consider this reality. If you kept your phone for twenty years, the manufacturers would only make an average of $50 a year. On the other hand, if these companies can make you feel the need to upgrade every two to three years, they raise their profit number to $300 to $500 annually. This is also why car companies bring out new models every year and clothes manufacturers make sure that styles are changing faster and faster.

You can find all kinds of products that used to be built to endure. Over time, companies have learned to design things to break down, to need an upgrade, or to go out of style. It is a marketing strategy that most of us don't notice as much as we should.

In the classic book *Charlie and the Chocolate Factory*, Willie Wonka invented a candy called the "Everlasting Gobstopper." This confectionary miracle could be enjoyed for weeks, months, and years and never melt away. However, even if a candy company today *could* make such a treat, the fact is that they *wouldn't*. It would put them out of business.

When it comes to marriage, it should endure like an Everlasting Gobstopper. Unfortunately, we have gotten used to things breaking down, going out of style, and needing an upgrade. When a marriage ends, we are becoming less and less surprised. When a couple throws in the towel, our world sees this as normal. But God wants us to flip the script and commit to building enduring marriages that last a lifetime—even when things are difficult.

1. Think about a couple you know who have stayed together through decades as they faced challenges, losses, and the daily reality of being married to an imperfect person. How has the couple's marriage become stronger through all they endured together?

Session Two: The Refining Power of Marriage

Timothy is a young pastor. His spiritual mentor, the apostle Paul, warns him that things in ministry are going to get wild at times. Sometimes you have to endure hardship. Paul calls him to press on and do what God called him to do. This same message should be heard by husbands and wives. We also have a ministry in our home. When things get crazy and difficult, don't freak out. Don't be surprised. And don't give up! Endure and remain faithful to do what God has called you to do. Marriage doesn't always make things better. It just makes things shared. Life isn't easy, so marriage won't be easy.

2. Read 2 Timothy 4:5. Describe a way you can do each of these things in the context of your marriage as you seek to endure the challenges of life:

> Stay calm, keep cool, and do not overreact . . .

> Stay strong and positive during the hard times in marriage . . .

> Do your unique part and fulfill your role in the family . . .

3. Read Romans 5:1–5. Notice the close connection between suffering, perseverance, character, and hope. How can enduring together as a couple actually bring hope into your marriage and home?

Sacred Marriage Bible Study

4. Think about a time you stood strong together as a couple. How does looking back on that season give you confident hope for the future?

Facing challenges as a couple can increase a sense of marital connection. Think about the things that lock hearts together for a lifetime. Soldiers who have fought in battle have a powerful connection. People who go on mission trips have a deep spiritual connection. Athletes who train together, compete side by side, and pour out every ounce of energy with their teammates forge a lasting bond. Going through dangers, difficulties, and deprivation can create a connection unlike anything else. The same is true for married couples who stand together through the hard times of life.

5. Read James 1:12. What is the reward promised to those who endure and stand strong through life's struggles and tests? How can remembering this hopeful truth inspire you and your spouse to endure as a couple through the hard seasons of marriage?

CATCH UP AND READ AHEAD

Take some time today to reflect on everything that you have learned this week. If you have been doing this study section on your own, connect with your spouse and discuss some of these key insights. Use any of the following prompts to help guide this time.

- When was a time of intense challenge you walked through in your marriage? Share some of the ways this journey has deepened your faith, strengthened your marriage, or brought you closer together.
- How have you grown more spiritually mature and drawn closer to Jesus because of difficulties you have faced in marriage?
- How can facing hard times with your spouse strengthen your marriage by deepening your faith?
- Jesus teaches that we will have trouble. He also calls us always to remember this profound truth: *He has overcome the world!* How does this truth bring hope and encouragement in the hard times?
- What are ways you can remind yourself and your spouse of the uplifting truth that Jesus has already overcome whatever you are going to face?

Use this time to go back and complete any of the study and reflection questions from previous days that you weren't able to finish. Make a note below of any revelations you've had and reflect on any growth or personal insights you've gained.

You may wish to review chapter 4 in *Sacred Marriage* before the next gathering group. Make note below of anything in that chapter that stands out to you or encourages you.

WEEK 3

BEFORE GROUP MEETING	Review chapter 4 in *Sacred Marriage* Read the Welcome section (page 38)
GROUP MEETING	Discuss the Connect questions Watch the video teaching for session 3 Discuss the questions that follow as a group Do the closing exercise and pray (pages 38–42)
STUDY 1	Complete the personal (or couple) study (pages 44–46)
STUDY 2	Complete the personal (or couple) study (pages 47–49)
STUDY 3	Complete the personal (or couple) study (pages 50–54)
CATCH UP & READ AHEAD (BEFORE WEEK 4 GROUP MEETING)	Review chapters 10–11 in *Sacred Marriage* Complete any unfinished personal studies (page 55)

SESSION THREE

THE GOD-CENTERED SPOUSE

God wants more for us in our marriage than we can imagine or dream. The way we get there is not by asking, "What do I want from my spouse," but "What does God want for both my spouse and me?"

WELCOME | READ ON YOUR OWN

Perhaps half of marriage is about motivation. Most of us know what we should do in an ideal marriage. The problem is that in the face of our spouse's stumbling (see James 3:2), we decide it's not worth the bother. Yet pulling back from our involvement in marriage because it doesn't complete us will make every marriage's demise inevitable.

We need more than romantic love to stay motivated in marriage. The average "shelf life" of an infatuation is 12 to 18 months. So what will keep us motivated to keep cherishing our spouse, loving our spouse, and moving toward our spouse when he or she disappoints us and the feelings fade—when all we're left with is a piece of paper that says we're supposed to stay married "until death do us part"?

We need a lifelong motivation that goes beyond our sin and infatuation—and the perfect place for a Christian to find that motivation is doing something out of reverence for God. God always deserves reverence. He is perfect, so there will be no sin to cancel out any contract. Our commitment to him is based on worship and his eternal worth, not on temporary romantic feelings or even the excellence of a spouse. When we learn to love our spouse out of reverence for *God*, we base our marriage on a lasting motivation that will not fade.

Allow your mind to dream about a marriage where the husband and wife focus on *Jesus* first—where they invite the Holy Spirit to empower and lead every decision. This approach to marriage can make the home a platform for increased worship. It can bring heaven to earth as the couple discovers the motivation they can never maintain on their own.

CONNECT | 10 MINUTES

Get this session started by choosing one or both of the following questions to discuss together as a group:

- What is something that spoke to you in last week's personal study that you would like to share with the group?

— *or* —

- Who were your primary examples and teachers (formally or informally) about what marriage should look like? What were the big lessons they taught you?

Session Three: The God-Centered Spouse

WATCH | 25 MINUTES

Now watch the video for this session. Below is an outline of the key points covered during the teaching. Record any key concepts that stand out to you.

OUTLINE

I. God is our good Father.
   A. Great memories of being a father.
   B. Through faith we are children of God (1 John 3:1).
   C. Our spouse is a loved child of the heavenly Father (Ephesians 5:1).
   D. If you want to get on my good side, love my kids.

II. God is a heavenly Father-in-law.
   A. When you marry a believer, you are being united to a child of God.
   B. You can please or anger the Father by how you treat your spouse.
   C. Loving your spouse out of reverence for God.
   D. A story about Lisa's dad.

III. Are we God-centered or spouse-centered in our marriage (Luke 6:32–36)?
   A. What's the difference?
   B. Loving an imperfect person.
   C. This is not a green light for any kind of abuse; on the contrary, it confronts and forbids abuse.
   D. Respect leads to spiritual growth (1 Peter 3:7).

IV. A new motivation for marriage (the *bema* seat of Christ; 2 Corinthians 5:10).
   A. This is not about getting to heaven.
   B. Well done, good and faithful servant.
   C. Motivated by God's goodness, not my spouse's performance.

NOTES

NOTES

Session Three: The God-Centered Spouse

DISCUSS | 35 MINUTES

Discuss what you just watched by answering the following questions.

1. Read 1 John 3:1–2 and Ephesians 5:1–2. What do these passages teach about how God wants you to see yourself and others? How might your interactions with others (including your spouse) change if you viewed every Christian as God's son or daughter?

2. If you see your spouse through God's eyes (your spouse's heavenly Father), how might that affect how patient you are with him or her? Or how quickly you extend forgiveness when he or she stumbles? Or how you speak words of blessing over your spouse?

3. Why is it so easy to slip into a me-centered approach in marriage? How can this be damaging and costly? How have you seen this happen in your marriage?

4. If God were to show up to your group in person and share a few reasons why he has such great love and affection for your spouse, what might he say? (Remember, your spouse is a loved and cherished child of God the Father!)

5. Ask someone to read Luke 6:32–33 and Matthew 5:43–46. What do you learn about love relationships from these passages? What do Jesus' teachings say to those who tend to give love to their spouses based on what their spouses do for them or how they feel about their spouses at any particular moment?

RESPOND | 10 MINUTES

God loves his children with perfect fatherly care. He is a provider and protector—far more than we recognize. One day in glory, God might show you all the ways he watched over you and delivered you through life (just the junor high years would be amazing to see!). He is with you at all times, and you are never alone. These truths should affect the way you see and treat yourself. It should also shape how you treat, love, and serve your spouse:

> See what great love the Father has lavished on us, that we should be called children of God! And that is what we are! The reason the world does not know us is that it did not know him. Dear friends, now we are children of God, and what we will be has not yet been made known. But we know that when Christ appears, we shall be like him, for we shall see him as he is.
>
> 1 JOHN 3:1-2

If you have children, how can the parental love and concern you have for your kids help you understand how God views his children?

How should these realities affect how we love, serve, and treat our spouse?

PRAY | 10 MINUTES

Ask God to help your focus be more on him and less on yourself or your spouse. Confess where you need to shift your heart more on God and less on yourself. Ask your heavenly Father to help you see your spouse more as his child than as your husband or wife. Finally, pray you will grow to be more and more like Jesus so you can love your spouse as he does.

SESSION THREE

PERSONAL (OR COUPLE) STUDY

Because we were made children of God through faith in Jesus, God is our heavenly Father. Most of us have a grasp on this. In the same way, if our *spouses* are followers of Jesus, they have also been adopted into God's family—so God is also their heavenly Father. Here is a new insight: *God is our Father-in-law*! He is watching over our spouses and cares more about how we love them than we can begin to comprehend. Keep this in mind as you work through the exercises. Write down your responses to the questions, as you will be given a few minutes to share your insights at the start of the next session if you are doing this study with others. If you are reading *Sacred Marriage* alongside this study, you may want to first review chapter 4 in the book.

STUDY 1

GOD AS YOUR HEAVENLY FATHER

The Bible uses Father language when speaking of God. Jesus used the intimate name Abba when speaking of the first person of the Trinity (see Mark 14:36). When he taught his disciples to pray, he told them to begin, "Our Father" (Matthew 6:9). Paul taught we are adopted into God's family through faith in Jesus and can cry out, "Abba, Father" (Romans 8:15). There is something powerful that happens in our souls when we realize we have a perfect, loving, powerful Father in heaven who engages tenderly with his children on earth.

Some people are reluctant to use *Father* language for God because they have bad memories of a harsh earthly father. Or they may be worried that other people will be pushed away from God if their earthly father was not a good presence in their life. The bottom line is that *every* earthly father is imperfect. The Bible uses this language to paint a picture of what we *long for* in a father: love, care, protection, provision and so much more.

It swells our souls when we realize our heavenly Father loves us. When we wake up in the morning, he is with us. As we walk through the day, his hand is always on us. While we care for family, as we play, and as we pray, our Father is near. Even when our hearts and minds wander where they should not be, the Father never leaves nor looks away.

He provides in amazing and miraculous ways. He protects us from things we see and even dangers we didn't know were there. Our Father is perfectly just and watches over us with a pure and godly jealousy that burns hot when others harm his beloved children. What a gift to know we are loved beyond our comprehension!

1. Read Mark 14:36, Romans 8:15, and Matthew 6:8. When you know you are a loved child of God, how should this affect the way you see and treat yourself?

Session Three: The God-Centered Spouse

2. It is important to realize the image of God as Father should not be based on your earthly father's weaknesses. Your heavenly Father is perfect in every way. Draw out some of the contrasts between earthly and heavenly fathers:

Earthly fathers can be . . .	But my heavenly father is always . . .

When we put our faith in Jesus, we are adopted into his family and become children of the living God. When I was a single man, the truth of that identity was so helpful in my faith. "I am God's beloved son. No one can take that away." I was even able to expand that truth to other believers. They are also children of God, which makes them my brothers and sisters. When we come to the cross and receive the grace of God revealed in the sacrifice of Jesus—when we confess our sins, take his hand, and follow Jesus as Lord—we are precious children of God.

3. Read Matthew 6:25–34. What pictures does Jesus use to show the various ways the Father looks out for his children?

Sacred Marriage Bible Study

4. How have you experienced the Father's love, provision, and protection over the past few months?

> God has loved me by . . .

> God has provided through . . .

> God protected me when . . .

God protects, provides, and watches over his kids, which should give us a sense of confidence. If you are a parent, think about the way you protect your children and how you want the best for them. When I became a dad, it was easy to get on my good side. *Just be kind to one of my kids.* In a similar way, if you wanted to get on my bad side, *just be mean to one of my kids.* I would much rather someone mess with me than my kids. God feels exactly the same way about us as his children!

5. What are ways you can thank, praise, and celebrate God for his Fatherly goodness and care in your life?

STUDY 2

GOD AS YOUR SPOUSE'S HEAVENLY FATHER

Have you ever had an *epiphany*? A brief definition of this rich word is "a sudden manifestation or perception of the essential nature or meaning of something." In other words, at the snap of a finger, you gain insight into something you never really comprehended or understood before.

This is an eye-opening, mind-expanding moment that can change your life.

Let's say a man named Bill has grown up with parents who taught him certain foods will lead to obesity, heart damage, or high cholesterol. Dad and Mom were not trying to freak him out but, in love, were trying to protect him. But over the years, fast food, sweets, and big portions have become the norm for Bill. He reads a few health books, listens to an occasional podcast, and even exercises a bit, but he keeps reverting to old patterns.

Bill puts on weight, gives up on exercise, and starts taking medications to manage the results of an unhealthy lifestyle. The years continue to pass. At one point, Bill goes in for his annual check-up. His doctor (a family friend) gives him a sober warning. He knows Bill just became a grandpa. With a solemn look, he says, "Bill, if you want to see your granddaughter grow up, you need to make some big changes!"

Bill suddenly has an epiphany: *My mom and dad were right.* He gets it! He is finally ready to change. And he does!

This session of *Sacred Marriage* offers the opportunity for you to have a marriage epiphany. Yes, you are a child of God, but—don't miss this—so is your spouse. This means God is your heavenly Father-in-law. God's love for your spouse is greater than yours. He cares about how you love, serve, and treat his child. If this does not wake you up to the need to love your spouse well, with kindness and grace, then you have a hard heart indeed.

So ask God to wake you up to this truth. It is time for a marriage epiphany!

○ Sacred Marriage Bible Study

1. When did you have an epiphany about something and your eyes were opened in a way that led to genuine life transformation?

> If you want to transform your marriage, meditate on God as your heavenly Father-in-law. From the day you say, "I do," this is your reality. When you recognize your spouse is also one of God's beloved children, it changes the way you look at being married to somebody who stumbles. In many ways, we all know our kids aren't perfect, but we're all praying that God will give them a patient, loving spouse. God wants the same, and he cares about how we treat each other.

2. If you were to have a marriage epiphany and recognize your spouse is a loved, cherished, and protected child of the heavenly Father . . .

What should you do more?

What should you stop doing (or at least do less)?

3. Reflect on a time when you withheld something from your spouse (such as communication, romance, affirmation, or serving) because your needs were unmet. How did your attitude and behavior affect your marriage? How do you think your heavenly Father-in-law felt about how you behaved toward your spouse?

Session Three: The God-Centered Spouse

4. Write down three ways you believe God (your heavenly Father-in-law) would want husbands to treat their wives. Then write down three ways you believe God (your heavenly Father-in-law) would want wives to treat their husbands.

How husbands should treat their wives . . .

1. _____
2. _____
3. _____

How wives should treat their husbands . . .

1. _____
2. _____
3. _____

What action can you take out of this exercise and imbed in your marriage?

Maybe when you got married you were so head over heels that you did not notice your fiancé stumbled in many ways. You missed that she had an attitude. You did not allow yourself to see that your husband-to-be had a bit of a temper. Years later you might feel like, "I didn't sign up for this." Now imagine your heavenly Father-in-law saying, "That's why I put you in your spouse's life. So you could love your spouse and walk with him or her through it all."

5. What do you think will be the result in your marriage if you begin to truly treat your spouse like a child of God and view God as your heavenly Father-in-law?

STUDY 3

GOD-CENTERED OR SPOUSE-CENTERED?

Have you ever found yourself watching a sporting competition that you know little about but that shows up every four years at the Olympics?

Maybe you were transfixed as men and women pushed large stones down a curling sheet of ice while teammates swept the ice and screamed commands. Or perhaps you started following your country's archery team and were struck by the staggering accuracy of these athletes as their arrows hit bullseye after bullseye.

If you watch these competitors closely—and if the camera work is done well—you can see the level of focus in these athletes' eyes is piercing. In each case, they are locked on the target with laser-like intensity. The reason for their focus is that the arrow or "rock" goes where they are looking. You will never see these athletes staring into space as they compete.

Focus means everything!

The same is true when it comes to marriage. Where we lock our eyes and focus our hearts reveals our true target. Keeping our attention on the right target leads to the best results. So here are the million-dollar questions: *Where should we focus in marriage? Who should we lock our eyes and hearts on to build the best future?* There are a few options.

First, we can focus on ourselves. If we do, we will get what we want and serve ourselves well . . . for a limited time. Second, we can focus on our spouses, treating them exactly like they treat us (which would be fine if they were perfect). Or, third, we can lock our eyes and hearts on the God who made and loves both us and our spouses.

If we do this, in his power, blessing can come to God, our spouses, and ourselves. This is God's design for marriage.

Session Three: The God-Centered Spouse

1. Where will each of these particular focuses in marriage lead?

> A marriage where you keep your eyes focused on you (your needs, desires, and dreams):

> A marriage where you respond to your spouse according to how he or she has recently responded to you:

> A marriage where you keep your eyes and heart focused on pleasing and worshiping God by loving his son or daughter well:

2. Consider the season of marriage that you are in right now. Where are your eyes primarily focused—on you, your spouse, or God—and what are some of the consequences?

> What are your eyes focused on right now?

> What are some of the consequences of this (either good or bad)?

Spouse-centered spouses treat the other person in the marriage based on how they have been treated in the past hours or days. If their spouse has been kind, thoughtful, and emotionally available, good things start flowing, patience is easy, and kindness is plentiful. If their spouse has been preoccupied, self-absorbed, short, or harsh, things do not go as well. It becomes a quid pro quo relationship. *You scratch my back, and I'll scratch yours. And, since you have not been scratching my back, guess what? You can scratch your own back for all I care.* Of course, few couples put it this bluntly, but this is the basic idea.

3. Read Matthew 5:38–42. How can a spouse-centered marriage become an eye-for-eye relationship? How does Jesus call his followers to a dramatically different kind of life?

Session Three: The God-Centered Spouse

4. Reflect on one or two of the areas of marriage listed in the table below. Write down some thoughts about how it would look if a person were being self-centered, spouse-centered, or God-centered in their approach to marriage.

Area of marriage	Self-centered	Spouse-centered	God-centered
How you handle finances			
How you forgive			
How you communicate			
How you express frustration			
How you use your free time			
How you navigate family of origin issues			
How you speak words of blessing			

What is one area you want to become more God-centered in how you relate to your spouse? What is a step forward you can take in your growth in this area?

The definition of Christian love is when we care for and serve those who take us for granted and even those who might be wicked toward us. Jesus teaches that if we can love those people, then we know his Spirit resides in us. It's that kind of love God offers us and calls us to extend to our spouses. The only possible way we can do this, over years and decades, is if it comes from God and we are staying God-centered.

5. How would your marriage change if you learned to love your spouse with the same consistency, kindness, and grace with which God loves you?

CATCH UP AND READ AHEAD

Take some time today to reflect on everything that you have learned this week. If you have been doing this study section on your own, connect with your spouse and discuss some of these key insights. Use any of the following prompts to help guide this time.

- How have you been viewing yourself as a loved child of your heavenly Father since you started doing this study?
- How have you been seeing and treating your spouse differently as you think of how the Father sees your spouse as his beloved child?
- What are some ways you have seen yourself respond from a self-centered or spouse-centered outlook?
- How have you been seeking to look at your spouse and marriage from a God-centered perspective? What impact is that making on your marriage?

Use this time to go back and complete any of the study and reflection questions from previous days that you weren't able to finish. Make a note below of any revelations you've had and reflect on any growth or personal insights you've gained.

You may wish to review chapters 10–11 in *Sacred Marriage* before the next gathering. Make note below of anything in those chapters that stands out to you or encourages you.

WEEK 4

BEFORE GROUP MEETING	Review chapters 10–11 in *Sacred Marriage* Read the Welcome section (page 58)
GROUP MEETING	Discuss the Connect questions Watch the video teaching for session 4 Discuss the questions that follow as a group Do the closing exercise and pray (pages 58–62)
STUDY 1	Complete the personal (or couple) study (pages 64–66)
STUDY 2	Complete the personal (or couple) study (pages 67–69)
STUDY 3	Complete the personal (or couple) study (pages 70–72)
CATCH UP & READ AHEAD (BEFORE WEEK 5 GROUP MEETING)	Review chapters 12–13 in *Sacred Marriage* Complete any unfinished personal studies (page 73)

SESSION FOUR

MARRIAGE: THE LOVE LABORATORY

When it comes to marriage, the message of our culture, media, novels, and often our own heart screams a singular message. . . . It is all about me being loved. God gently whispers a radically different story . . . marriage is about you learning to love, beginning with your spouse. Here is the million-dollar question: "What message is shaping your marriage?"

○ Sacred Marriage Bible Study

WELCOME | READ ON YOUR OWN

If you go to a gym and tell a trainer you want to strengthen your upper body, you will be put on a program to build up your core, biceps, abs, and back. It will be hard, but if you stick with the program for a few months, you will see and feel a profound difference.

Imagine getting news from your doctor that you have high blood pressure. You ask for insight on how to lower it without taking medications. The doctor says, "It is going to demand hard work in a number of areas. Get ready to change your diet, increase your physical activity, drop some pounds, manage your stress levels, and increase your sleep."

Your boss lets you know that she loves your work and values having you on the team. She wants to increase your responsibility and pay, but it is going to mean you need to learn a new language so you can offer leadership in a country where your company does a lot of business. They will pay for the classes, but you need to do the work. It will mean a year of night school, tons of memorization, study, and extra time.

The bottom line? Almost everything in life that is valuable demands hard work, sacrifice, and consistent effort. There is a way to get there, but you must do the workout, follow your doctor's orders, and attend class. Now imagine you are standing before God. You ask, "How can I grow into a more loving person?" His answer surprises you: "Get married and give it all you have." Marriage is a divinely designed *love laboratory*. If you follow God's instructions for marriage, you will discover what it truly means to love.

CONNECT | 15 MINUTES

Get this session started by choosing one or both of the following questions to discuss together as a group:

- What is something that spoke to you in last week's personal study that you would like to share with the group?

— *or* —

- How has being married taught you how to love and serve in ways you never experienced before?

Session Four: Marriage: The Love Laboratory

WATCH | 20 MINUTES

Now watch the video for this session. Below is an outline of the key points covered during the teaching. Record any key concepts that stand out to you.

OUTLINE

I. God's design was to make us different.
   A. The power of opposites.
   B. Jesus was a pioneer in calling people to love (Matthew 22:34–40).
   C. Love is learned, again and again.
II. Christianity = Love (1 John 4:20–21).
   A. Why did you get married? Honestly?
   B. Love is our greatest need (Colossians 3:14; 1 Peter 4:8).
   C. Love is a command (John 13:34).
   D. Love tells a story.
   E. Love is a biblical calling (Titus 2:4; Ephesians 5:25).
III. Marriage is the perfect love laboratory.
   A. A laboratory to learn epic sacrifice (Chris and Stefanie's Story).
   B. A laboratory for putting your spouse first (Gary and Lisa's story).
   C. A laboratory for intimacy and healing (Caleb and Krista's story).
   D. Once we are in Christ, our greatest need is to learn how to love.

NOTES

Sacred Marriage Bible Study

NOTES

Session Four: Marriage: The Love Laboratory

DISCUSS | 35 MINUTES

Discuss what you just watched by answering the following questions.

1. Ask someone to read aloud Genesis 2:15–25. What do you learn about God's personal engagement with his creation of man and woman? How should God's delight and design affect the way you see the goodness of male and female?

2. Now ask someone to read Colossians 3:12–14 and 1 Peter 4:8. The Bible teaches that love holds things together, covers sin, and accomplishes God's purposes. Why do you think the Bible focuses so much on the theme of treating other people with love?

3. Tell about a time you watched a husband love his wife well. What did he say and do that made you think, *This man loves his wife*? Share an account of a time you watched a wife love her husband in such a way that you could not miss or deny the presence of love in their relationship. How was God glorified in that expression of love?

4. Invite someone to read Titus 2:3–5 and Ephesians 5:25. In our culture, we are trained to think of love as a spontaneous emotion, but the Bible teaches that love is a command to follow. What lesson, if any, did someone teach you about loving and caring for your spouse? Have you ever made a serious effort to love and serve your spouse—and God showed up in a meaningful way? Explain what happened.

5. When you hear stories of loving sacrifice in marriage, like the ones shared in this week's teaching, how does that inspire you to love your spouse with greater devotion? What is one step forward in devoted and sacrificial love that you believe God wants you to take in the coming weeks? How will you actually take that step?

RESPOND | 10 MINUTES

First Corinthians 13 is often called the love chapter. It is read at weddings and is filled with powerful images of how one person can show love to another. It also points out what love is *not*. This passage falls in the middle of the apostle Paul's teaching on community in the church. It can easily be applied to a church, a family, a group of Christian friends, and many other gatherings of believers. It can also certainly, with theological integrity, speak to one of the most intimate relationships between two believers: *marriage*.

> Love is patient, love is kind. It does not envy, it does not boast, it is not proud. It does not dishonor others, it is not self-seeking, it is not easily angered, it keeps no record of wrongs. Love does not delight in evil but rejoices with the truth. It always protects, always trusts, always hopes, always perseveres.
>
> 1 CORINTHIANS 13:4–7

What is one characteristic of love addressed by Paul that you want to live out more consistently in your marriage?

How can focusing on loving your spouse instead of focusing on how your spouse loves you change the dynamic in your marriage for the better?

PRAY | 10 MINUTES

Thank God for the people in your life who are examples of love in marriage that continues through the years with the ups and downs of life. Ask God to change your thinking about marriage from being focused on how you can be loved to how God wants you to love your spouse. Pray for your group members to endure and be patient with each other as they learn how to love. Finally, pray for love that forgives quickly and looks over offenses.

SESSION FOUR

PERSONAL (OR COUPLE) STUDY

One of the best settings for believers in Christ to grow in love, learn about God's love, and be shaped into a person whose life is marked by love is . . . *marriage*. There are few other areas that will stretch your patience, demand your service, crucify your selfishness, or bring you to your knees in prayer. When you say, "I do," you step into what could be called the "love laboratory." Keep this in mind as you work through the exercises. Write down your responses to the questions, as you will be given a few minutes to share your insights at the start of the next session if you are doing this study with others. If you are reading *Sacred Marriage* alongside this study, you may want to first review chapters 10–11 in the book.

STUDY 1

GOD'S DESIGN OF DIFFERENCES

The God we worship is the most creative being in the universe! Take a moment and look up "naked mole rat" online. This unique creature is sometimes called a sand puppy and is a hairless burrowing rodent native to the Horn of Africa. Do a quick search on the "Australian walking stick." This insect has a stunning ability to hide in plain sight. From penguins to puppies, from katydids to kittens, the Maker of heaven and earth is endlessly innovative.

When it comes to human beings, God made men and women in his image. There are many ways men and women are similar in our divine design, but there are also distinct ways we are dramatically different. These differences are wonderful, beautiful, and sometimes challenging. In a powerful and mysterious way, men and women together reflect the image of glory in a way that just one gender would not.

These heavenly designed differences challenge, stretch, and sharpen us. A husband can be made better over time because of his wife's differences if he is humble and invites God to work through his bride. A wife can mature when she welcomes her husband's differences and sees them as part of God's plan. Rather than driving us away from each other, honestly facing our differences, blessing them, learning from them, and then discovering how facing our differences can make each other more like Jesus can bind the hearts of a husband and wife together. At the same time, they can come closer to God than they ever have before.

A thoughtful husband once said, "If my wife and I were identical, one of us would be unnecessary . . . and I'm pretty sure it would be me!" Thankfully, we are different by design. God uses this to grow every married person who embraces the way God has made them.

1. What is a specific way you and your spouse are different? How has God used this difference to make both of you better people and followers of Jesus?

Session Four: Marriage: The Love Laboratory

2. Read Matthew 22:34–40. How can a deep and growing love for God help you see and embrace your spouse's differences in the following ways?

Physically:

Emotionally:

Spiritually:

If God's intention for marriage was to create a relationship in which we would always be happy, never face conflict, and have eternally smooth sailing, why did he design two people who are so different? Neuroscience teaches us about fundamental differences between the male and female brains. We have family of origin differences. We enter marriage with varied dreams, desires, motivations, physiology, and energy levels. On the other hand, if God's design for marriage was to take two people who stumble in many ways and teach them how to love someone who is dramatically different and who looks at the world from another perspective, I can't imagine a better invention than marriage.

3. What are some differences between you and your spouse that you have discovered along the course of your marriage? How have these differences changed over time?

○ Sacred Marriage Bible Study

4. What are three ways you are different from your spouse? How could God could use these differences to strengthen each of you if you affirm and celebrate them?

Difference #1: _____

How God could use this to strengthen and help you and your spouse:

Difference #2: _____

How God could use this to strengthen and help you and your spouse:

Difference #3: _____

How God could use this to strengthen and help you and your spouse:

Take time to share this with your spouse and pray that God will use your differences to make you more like Jesus and strengthen your marriage over time.

Love is a lesson to be learned more than a feeling to be felt. Jesus wants us to love like he did. His love was sacrificial, not self-centered and demanding. No human being needs to read a book to learn how to be selfish. We don't need to go to a seminar to learn how to hold a grudge. Those negative things come naturally. But if we want to learn how to love the way that Jesus describes love, it's a lesson we have to learn again and again and again. This is why marriage is such a great place to learn to love. It gives us a chance *dozens* of times every day to choose love.

5. What is one of your recurring marriage challenges that is based on a fundamental difference between you and your spouse? How is facing this difference again and again in your marriage stretching you to be more like Jesus?

66

STUDY 2

CHRISTIANITY = LOVE

Imagine you are in a class and are given a card with this equation on it:

CHRISTIANITY = _____

You are asked to finish the equation by filling in the blank with one word. You would likely receive a number of answers from class members:

CHRISTIANITY = _doctrine_
CHRISTIANITY = _kindness_
CHRISTIANITY = _faith_
CHRISTIANITY = _judgmentalism_

People have divergent ideas. Yes, *doctrine* is an important part of the Christian faith. *Kindness* is a supernatural by-product of the presence of the Holy Spirit. *Faith* is required for someone to enter a relationship with Jesus. And, sadly, some people's perception of Christian believers is that of casting *judgment* on anyone who does not belong to their club.

But based on the the teaching and life of our Savior, we can be pretty confident how Jesus would finish the equation:

CHRISTIANITY = _love_

God so loved the world that he gave his only Son (see John 3:16). When asked what was the greatest commandment, Jesus said that loving God with all we are and loving our neighbor summarized all the Law and the Prophets (see Matthew 22:34–40). Jesus prophetically told his followers there was no greater love than to lay down their lives for friends, and then he died on the cross for us (see John 15:13). Love is the center of Christianity.

1. How did Jesus model love, teach about love, and call his followers to live in love?

○ Sacred Marriage Bible Study

2. Read Matthew 22:34–40. How does love for God empower you to love other people? How does loving other people grow your love for the God who made them?

Love in marriage should be more about serving than being served. It should be more about lifting up our spouse than finding someone to meet our needs. But let's be honest. Most of us get married because of what we think we will gain from our spouse. When I got married, I thought my greatest need was to be loved. Now I know that God looked at my needs from an entirely different perspective. Once you have received the *Father's* love, your greatest need for love has already been fulfilled. Once you are in a relationship with Jesus, your greatest need is to learn how to love others—and on the top of the list of people to love is your spouse.

3. Read 1 John 4:19–21. Think about what drives people to get married. When men or women decide they have met their future spouses, what is it that "seals the deal"? Consider this in terms of a me-centered approach and a Christ-centered approach.

> *I want to marry that person because he or she will . . .*

> *I have the honor of marrying this person so that in the power of Jesus I can love them by . . .*

Session Four: Marriage: The Love Laboratory

4. Read Colossians 3:12–14 and 1 Peter 1:7–8. What does it mean for you and your spouse to clothe yourselves with love and love each other deeply? What could this look like in your marriage?

When Paul writes to the Colossian church, he challenges them to wear love like a garment, because this binds everything together in harmony. The church in Colossae was a young Christian community. Most of them had been Christians for only a matter of months, not years. So Paul is giving them a number of specific ethical guidelines. When he sums it all up, he calls them to love one another. It is interesting that Peter says essentially the same thing. He calls believers to deep levels of love and reminds them of the healing power that is unleashed when we extend God's love to each other.

5. What is one way you can seek to love your spouse, in increasing measure, in each of these areas of your relationship?

Showing love to your spouse through growing *spiritual* engagement . . .

Showing love to your spouse *physically* . . .

Showing love to your spouse *emotionally* and *relationally* . . .

STUDY 3

THE PERFECT LABORATORY FOR LOVE

If you want to see a place designed for the building and development of electric vehicles, consider the Tesla Gigafactory outside Austin, Texas. The floor area is over 10,000,000 square feet. The plant can function with 20,000 employees working. Imagine what that kind of brain power, muscle, and creative energy could come up with as it relates to cars.

Or consider chocolate bars. In 1847, Joseph Fry, a British confectioner, made the first commercial edible chocolate bar. He did so through trial and error in a chocolate laboratory, in the process giving a gift to the world. It was called "Fry's Chocolate Cream Bar."

There are laboratories for electric cars, chocolate bars, and just about anything you can imagine . . . and even some things you can't. But what if you asked God, "What is a great laboratory for *love*?" One answer would be *marriage*. In the covenant of marriage, instituted by God, we can learn more about love than almost anywhere else.

Consider some of the experiments God might invite you to participate in as you step into the marriage love laboratory. How do you take two very different people, who stumble in many ways, and help them love God and each other enough to forgive the past and keep loving each other in the future? How do you bless and affirm a person who sees the world differently than you do and honor his or her perspective (even if you don't always agree)? How do you lovingly serve someone when you are exhausted, empty, and feeling like you need someone to care for you? How do you set aside your wants, desires, and sometimes your dreams for the sake of helping your spouse fulfill God's call on his or her life?

These kinds of experiments can make us more like Jesus and teach us to love others the way Jesus loves us.

1. What is one experiment of sacrificial love that God has invited you to participate in since you got married? How did this make you more like Jesus?

70

Session Four: Marriage: The Love Laboratory

2. What are three things you chose to give up for the sake of loving your spouse? What have you learned, how have you grown, and what have you received as a result?

As you gave up this . . .   you learned, grew, or received this . . .

_____   _____

As you gave up this . . .   you learned, grew, or received this . . .

_____   _____

As you gave up this . . .   you learned, grew, or received this . . .

_____   _____

Marriage has been artfully designed by God to get our attention, wake us up, pinch our feet. You married an imperfect person. Accept it. And you are not the perfect spouse . . . but you already know that! Being married to somebody who stumbles in many ways is a perfect opportunity to learn how to love. Most of us did not get married thinking God would use it as a laboratory to grow us, challenge us, and help us earn an advanced degree in loving others like Jesus does. But here we are! So let's make the most of our love laboratory and ask God to empower us in this exciting adventure.

3. On a scale of 1 to 10 (1 being not at all and 10 being all the time), where are you when it comes to actively working at loving your spouse with intentional and consistent acts of loving service? (Consider how you can raise this up one or two notches!)

○———○———○———○———○———○———○———○———○———○

[Not at all]   [All the time]

○ Sacred Marriage Bible Study

4. Read Ephesians 5:21–33. In this passage, the apostle Paul gives a high calling to both the husband and wife. Why is mutual submission to each other essential for us to live out this call? What is one step forward you can take in submission to your spouse out of reverence for Jesus?

Sometimes the words of a song can sneak up on you and catch your attention. I was listening to the radio and the lyrics of Amy Grant's song "Like I Love You from Behind the Eyes" struck me. The grammar can be excused, but the message should make us stop and think: "Ain't nobody gonna say goodbye. No, ain't nobody gonna walk away. This time, baby, I'm learning how to love you, love you." What a reminder of the high calling we have! Every day we can wake up and pray, "Lord of heaven, help me love my spouse today more than they have dreamed and more than I ever could in my own power."

5. If someone asked your spouse, "What is one way your spouse could love you with more consistency and impact?" what do you think your spouse would say? How might you begin doing this before your spouse has to ask you?

CATCH UP AND READ AHEAD

Take some time today to reflect on everything that you have learned this week. If you have been doing this study section on your own, connect with your spouse and discuss some of these key insights. Use any of the following prompts to help guide this time.

- What are you learning about love in the laboratory of your marriage?
- What is one way you and your spouse are opposites? How does this stretch you and grow you in your faith?
- Where do you need to grow in sacrificial love toward your spouse? How can others pray for you as you seek to be more like Jesus in this area of your life?
- Colossians 3:14 calls you to dress yourself in love more than any other virtue. What is one thing you could do at the start of each day that would show your spouse that you are seeking to actively love him or her?
- Colossians 3:13 reveals God's desire to forgive others in the same manner that Jesus forgave us. How are you doing in following this exhortation? How do you need to grow in this area of your marriage?

Use this time to go back and complete any of the study and reflection questions from previous days that you weren't able to finish. Make a note below of any revelations you've had and reflect on any growth or personal insights you've gained.

You may wish to review chapters 12–13 in *Sacred Marriage* before the next gathering. Make note below of anything in those chapters that stands out to you or encourages you.

WEEK 5

BEFORE GROUP MEETING	Review chapters 12–13 in *Sacred Marriage* Read the Welcome section (page 76)
GROUP MEETING	Discuss the Connect questions Watch the video teaching for session 5 Discuss the questions that follow as a group Do the closing exercise and pray (pages 76–80)
STUDY 1	Complete the personal (or couple) study (pages 82–84)
STUDY 2	Complete the personal (or couple) study (pages 85–87)
STUDY 3	Complete the personal (or couple) study (pages 88–90)
CATCH UP & READ AHEAD (BEFORE WEEK 6 GROUP MEETING)	Review chapters 8–9 and 14 in *Sacred Marriage* Complete any unfinished personal studies (page 91)

SESSION FIVE

SEXUAL SAINTS

In a sexually confused and broken world, believers in Jesus need to reclaim God's good plan for sexuality, celebrate the beautiful gift of being male and female, and model what it means to be sexual saints.

Sacred Marriage Bible Study

WELCOME | READ ON YOUR OWN

We all agree Bible study is good, valuable, and fruitful in the life of a Christian. When it comes to prayer, we are all on the same page. Talking with God, lifting up our needs, and praising our Maker should be an important part of our lives. These are simple and fundamental areas of agreement among the people of Jesus.

Then there are topics that push some people's buttons. On the top of this list, for many people, is sex, physical intimacy, romantic love, and all of the related activities. For some reason, this God-ordained gift can bring confusion and conflict. How should a Christian view sexuality? How should holiness-seeking saints of God feel about a man and woman, in the context of a marriage covenant, intertwining their bodies and souls in passionate sexual intimacy? And how does God feel about this complex and contested topic?

The bottom line is this: *God is a fan of sex.* He invented it. He declared it "very good" (see Genesis 1:31)! When it comes to the uniqueness of men and women, including their sexuality, God loves it. As to the topic of sexual intimacy between a woman and a man within the boundaries God has established, the Maker of heaven delights in it.

One of the calls on God's people is to reclaim the gifts God has given us. On the top of that list is being sexual saints. It is time for us to see sexuality through the eyes of the God who invented it. This is our moment to embrace the goodness of male and female, the oneness of God-honoring sexual intimacy, and the privilege of living as sexual saints.

CONNECT | 15 MINUTES

Get this session started by choosing one or both of the following questions to discuss together as a group:

- What is something that spoke to you in last week's personal study that you would like to share with the group?

— *or* —

- What was your outlook on sexuality as you were growing up and what factors shaped your perspective on this complex and often painful topic?

Session Five: Sexual Saints

WATCH | 20 MINUTES

Now watch the video for this session. Below is an outline of the key points covered during the teaching. Record any key concepts that stand out to you.

OUTLINE

I. The best source of teaching on sexuality.
   A. A magazine article.
   B. The Bible: Song of Songs.
   C. The design of God.
II. The gift of sexual intimacy for her.
   A. Three thousand years ago, wine was on the top of the list.
   B. Sex can be better than wine.
   C. The Bible expects that married sex is a gift to a wife (1 Corinthians 7:4–5).
   D. Husbands should prioritize their wife's sexual pleasure.
III. The gift of sexual intimacy for him.
   A. A biblical picture of being fired up sexually (Song of Songs 1:9).
   B. Sexual intimacy feeds a man's eyes, body, and soul (Proverbs 5:18–19).
   C. Enjoy morally permissible love ecstasy.
   D. Sexual intimacy can become all-consuming in the moment.
IV. God's perspective on sex.
   A. God delights in his invention of male, female, and sexuality.
   B. God's design of the male and female brain affirms his delight.
   C. A godly sexual life as a couple leads to spiritual maturity.
   D. Spiritual maturity and love lead to greater satisfaction in our sexual relationship.

NOTES

NOTES

Session Five: Sexual Saints

DISCUSS | 35 MINUTES

Discuss what you just watched by answering the following questions.

1. Ask someone to read aloud Song of Songs 1:1–9 and 1 Corinthians 7:3–5. What does the Bible teach about the gift of sexual pleasure for a husband and wife? Why is it important for both parties to take God's design for mutual satisfaction seriously during times of sexual intimacy?

2. Now read Proverbs 5:18–19 and Song of Songs 1:16. How does God feel about the marriage relationship when it comes to a man and wife having sexual intimacy? In light of this, what would you say to a Christian who says, "I think God is against sex and truly holy Christians won't prioritize regular sexual activities"?

3. Consistent spiritual growth in marriage partners leads naturally to an increasingly vibrant and healthy sexual relationship. How could these Christian virtues and biblical callings strengthen a marriage on every level, including not only *sexually* but also in the areas of *forgiving* each other, showing *empathy*, and demonstrating *sacrifice*?

4. Like a canary in the coal mine, there are warning signs when sexual intimacy is waning. What are some of the warning signs you think married couples should watch for? How should you take these seriously and overcome the challenges you might face?

5. Every season of marriage presents its own hurdles, so you are wise to plan in advance to nurture intimacy through every chapter of married life. What are ways couples can invest in their marriage by nurturing intentional romance and Jesus-honoring sexual intimacy in (1) the newlywed season, (2) when the first child comes along, (3) when raising kids during the "taxi service" years, and (4) in the later years of life?

○ Sacred Marriage Bible Study

RESPOND | 10 MINUTES

The structure of Song of Songs includes "she says" portions, "he says" sections, and even an occasional appearance of a community of friends celebrating God's good gift of sexual intimacy. Read the following passage from Song of Songs together and use the question below to guide your conversation. Take note when "he" is speaking and when "she" is speaking.

> **She:** Let him kiss me with the kisses of his mouth—for your love is more delightful than wine. Pleasing is the fragrance of your perfumes; your name is like perfume poured out. No wonder the young women love you! Take me away with you—let us hurry! Let the king bring me into his chambers. . . .
>
> **He:** I liken you, my darling, to a mare among Pharaoh's chariot horses. Your cheeks are beautiful with earrings, your neck with strings of jewels. We will make you earrings of gold, studded with silver.
>
> SONG OF SONGS 1:2–4, 9–11

What do you learn about the husband's passion and feelings for his wife? What do you learn about the wife's passion and feelings for her husband?

What lessons can we learn about being expressive to our spouse about our love, admiration, and passion for them?

PRAY | 10 MINUTES

Thank God for his good plan of creating us male and female and the gift of physical intimacy in marriage. Ask for a heart to fully embrace God's good plan of sexuality and pray for correction in your thinking if your perspective on sex and intimacy is not in line with God's Word. Finally, ask the Holy Spirit to help you grow the following virtues in your life and marriage: forgiveness, empathy, kindness, generosity, sacrifice . . . and whatever else God places on your heart.

SESSION FIVE

PERSONAL (OR COUPLE) STUDY

We turned up the temperature a bit in this session by focusing on physical and sexual intimacy. We explored how God designed these and how they are celebrated by our Creator (when they are expressed in the context God designed them). For some people, this is a painful topic. For others, it is uncomfortable. For God, it is simply part of his plan for intimacy and spiritual growth. No matter your starting point on this topic, God wants you to adopt his perspective and grow to appreciate the good gift of this sacred expression. As you work through the exercises, write down your responses to the questions, as you will be given a few minutes to share your insights at the start of the next session if you are doing this study with others. If you are reading *Sacred Marriage* alongside this study, you may first want to review chapters 12–13 in the book.

STUDY 1

GO TO THE SOURCE

Where do you go when you want real wisdom and solid answers to life's questions? Many would say Google, Chat GPT, or some sort of AI are the best and most accessible sources of good information. To be sure, when you are looking for things like the winner of the 1969 World Series, or a few paragraphs describing World War II, computer-generated descriptions can be quick and helpful. But we need to be careful to read these answers with a grain of salt and some thoughtful discernment.

This is because when it comes to finding insight into complex human engagement such as sexuality, we need to *be wary*. Even if a computer can gather data and synthesize it, there will be lots of influence based on who set up the algorithm. Morality and divine direction are not factored into an AI-generated answer to these kinds of questions.

When it comes to understanding sex in marriage (and the proper way to understand our sexuality outside of marriage), we need to go to the source. God is the inventor of men and women, and of the two becoming one in a sexual fusion of body, heart, and soul. God defines the proper context for the expression of sexual desires. Our Creator brought together a man and a woman and said, "Be fruitful and multiply" (Genesis 1:28 ESV).

Sadly, many Christians draw their understanding and view of sexuality from the world rather than from heaven. Too many followers of Jesus are walking the path set by culture rather than God's clear and life-giving road. Tragically, many men, and a growing number of women, have been tainted by pornography and have a hard time purging their mind of damaging images and their heart of damaging ideas.

Our God is not shy when it comes to this topic. He invented sex. Let's go to the source for the best answers on this deeply important topic.

1. Whether you grew up in church and a Christian family or in a non-faith-oriented environment, you had sources of learning and insight regarding sex. For better or worse, you got your information about sex from movies, friends, TV, family, school teachers, youth pastors, the Bible . . . the list goes on. What were your primary sources

Session Five: Sexual Saints

of learning, and how biblically accurate or inaccurate were they? List three potential sources and mark where you feel they fall on the scale of being biblically accurate.

Source: _____

○——○——○——○——○——○——○——○——○——○

[Unbiblical]   [Some biblical roots]   [Very biblical]

Source: _____

○——○——○——○——○——○——○——○——○——○

[Unbiblical]   [Some biblical roots]   [Very biblical]

Source: _____

○——○——○——○——○——○——○——○——○——○

[Unbiblical]   [Some biblical roots]   [Very biblical]

2. When you are looking for relational wisdom for marriage (including complex topics like sexuality), who do you call on with a high level of confidence that they will give valuable and biblical insight? Why is it important to have people in your life like this?

If you have any doubt that God is our best source of truth about sex, just look at the Bible. It is the only subject that gets its own book in Scripture. As important as prayer is to the Christian life, there isn't a single book of the Bible devoted exclusively to prayer. As important as giving and handling our money wisely are to God, there isn't a single book in the Bible devoted exclusively to finances. But there is one book in the Bible—the Song of Songs—devoted exclusively to the sexual relationship between a husband and a wife. That should tell us how important this topic is to God and direct us to turn our eyes to the Bible when we want to understand this glorious and mysterious topic.

Sacred Marriage Bible Study

3. On almost every topic related to our sexuality, biblical teaching stands in stark contrast to what the modern world says. What are some of these contrasts?

4. Read Song of Songs 5:1. How can we celebrate and hold to God's design and plan for us as sexual people?

In the ancient world, if you said, "God is the King of kings," it did not mean he was the greatest of kings, or the wisest of kings, or the strongest of kings. It meant that if you were to put *all* the kings of the universe together, God would be King of those kings. Think about this in terms of the title "Song of Songs." It means there is no other song like this song. Given that God devotes a whole book of the Bible to this important topic, we need to commit ourselves to learn all we can about sex from the God who invented it and lifts it up.

5. What are ways you can dig deeper into this topic in the Bible and learn from godly Christians who take God's Word very seriously?

For more information on this topic, see Gary Thomas and Debra Fileta, *Married Sex: A Christian Couple's Guide to Reimagining Your Love Life* (Zondervan, 2021).

STUDY 2

PLEASURE FOR ALL

Just how much physical, sexual pleasure does God want married couples to experience? In this week's teaching, you discussed how God invented male, female, and sex. But are Christians really meant to focus on pleasure? After all, Jesus called his followers to "deny themselves and take up their cross" (Matthew 16:24). Ascetics through the ages have rejected bodily gratification, and some have even punished their body "for the glory of God." How should devoted believers in Jesus understand the topic of pleasure?

Perspective #1: Christians should appreciate God's good gifts of every kind, but don't overdo it. Good food is fine, but don't be a glutton! Sex is fine, but use some restraint and moderation. Once you have kids, sex is fine, but it should not be a focal point of a married couple's life. Focus on spiritual pursuits and not things of the flesh. Let's not invest too much time thinking about, or engaging in, sexual intimacy. Pleasure is overrated and mature Christians will not let this be a focal point of their life.

Perspective #2: Christians should make their romantic and sexual life a source of joy and intimacy. Sex is good. Pleasure is a gift. So, enjoy sexual pleasure for your good and the glory of God. But remember, God's greatest concern is the soul, not the body. When you engage in spiritual pursuits, God delights! When we are focused on physical pleasure, enjoy it but know that this is not the purpose of your life or the main thing you should invest in.

Perspective #3: Christians should lead the way in sexual intimacy, enjoyment, and celebration. Our Maker designed our brains, bodies, hearts, chemical makeup, and sense of touch to fully engage in sexual expression with our spouse. Of all the people on the planet, Christians have it right! The bedroom and sex can be a training ground for godliness and transformation. Sexual expression is God's domain, so enjoy it fully, enthusiastically, and often!

1. Which of these perspectives reflects your understanding of Christian sexuality? Why? (If none of these accurately reflects your view, create a fourth perspective.)

○ Sacred Marriage Bible Study

2. Read Song of Songs 2:14 and 4:1–2. God designed us to capture the attention of our spouses and draw them to us. How can tender and cherishing words draw the attention of our spouses and set the stage for intimate connection?

There were few pleasures for women three thousand years ago. One that did exist was enjoying the taste and effect of a glass of wine. So when we read the words of a woman declaring, "For your love is more delightful than wine" (Song of Songs 1:2), we recognize she is telling her husband that sexual intimacy with him is better than the best man-made pleasure she can think of. The Bible celebrates and sanctifies the pleasure women get from sex. It is not just for the husband. This passage stresses that sex was created for the wife and the husband as one of life's highest pleasures.

3. When it comes to the Christian faith and God's design of male and female, most of us don't start pondering the recent finds of neuroscience. But there are fascinating insights that can help shape our view of ourselves and our spouse. What insights about the male and female brain did you receive from this week's teaching? How should those divinely designed realities affect the way you see yourself and your spouse in the realm of sexuality?

Session Five: Sexual Saints

4. You might want to use the following questions to talk as a couple and identify possible blind spots in your relationship. Check the box for each one you will discuss.

☐ Is there anything that is damaging our sexual relationship?

☐ Are we making romance a priority? If not, how can we pay attention to this?

☐ Are there any sources of sexual repression in how we think God views a sexual relationship? If so, where is this coming from and how can it be corrected?

☐ Is one of us being selfish in life in general or in our sexual relationship specifically?

☐ Are either of us too tired or too busy? How is this affecting the romance part of our relationship?

☐ What is keeping our sexual relationship from flourishing and being all God created it to be? How might we remove this obstacle?

In Proverbs 5:18, a husband is exhorted to rejoice in his wife. In the Bible, this word *rejoice* often means to clap, dance, and shout with joy. These are powerful images! But in this context, it relates to how a husband responds when he sees the fullness of his wife's physical beauty. In Proverbs 5:19, we find the Hebrew word for *captivated*, which has been described as "morally permissible love ecstasy." At that moment, nothing else exists for him. He doesn't remember if he likes his job or hates it. He doesn't think about if he's wealthy or poor. All he wants is right there in front of him. He is captivated.

5. Read Proverbs 5:15–20. This picture of water and drinking deeply is clearly about sexual intimacy. How does this passage affirm and celebrate the goodness of God's amazing gift of married sex?

STUDY 3

SACRED SEXUALITY

Satan wants to corrupt every good gift our heavenly Father has lavished on us. Just think about it. God invented the taste of a freshly picked apple. God has given us creativity to take the amazing ingredients he has given in nature to make so many different dishes that bear the name of an entire country or people group. We can go out for Italian food, Korean BBQ, Mexican food, and the like. What a gift God has given! Yet the enemy loves to steal, kill, and destroy (see John 10:10). Gluttony and selfishness can eclipse the wonderful gift of food if we listen to the enticements of the enemy of our soul.

Our words can bless and build up but they can also burn and tear down if they are not surrendered to the power of the Holy Spirit (see James 3:9–12). Our speech can be used to encourage, bless, preach, sing, and give glory to God. But when the enemy gets into our heart, mind, and mouth, the tongue can bring profound destruction. Most people can remember words of blessing and words of cursing from early in their childhood as if it were yesterday.

Every good gift can be corrupted and few have been more twisted than sexuality.

God made sex holy and sacred. A gift like no other. But Satan wants to make it profane and damaging. What is meant to warm our soul and ignite our passion for our spouses can burn and devastate us and others. Our sexuality was originally the domain of our loving and kind God. It is time for followers of Jesus to step into God's plan and fully enjoy this good gift in the setting it was designed to thrive.

1. What are ways the enemy has tried to confuse people about sexuality and steal the good gift that God designed? How do we battle against this work of the enemy?

Session Five: Sexual Saints

2. What are some ways the enemy tries to keep a husband and wife from enjoying intimacy, romance, and sexual expression? How can you avoid these roadblocks?

Roadblock to intimacy	How to avoid this roadblock

> God urges married men and women to give their selves over to the wonderful experience he created. The sexual intimacy described in the Song of Songs is beautifully shocking. It is a picture of a woman saying that when her husband makes love to her, it is better than the best pleasure she could imagine. The husband's desire for his wife is compared to a stallion's sexual frenzy when a mare is close by. When a husband and wife see each other as God designed and intended, they are intoxicated with passion for each other. This is the message from God's Word.

3. Discuss the following with your spouse this week and write down the responses.

Are there any ways you see me dishonoring you or treating you in a way that does not exemplify the grace and kindness of Jesus?

Sacred Marriage Bible Study

> What is one suggestion you could give me to really tend to the romantic part of our marriage?

4. What is one positive step you and your spouse could take as a couple to increase the romance and intimacy in your marriage? How will you make sure this happens?

There are simple shifts we can make in how we behave, speak, act, and think about our spouse. Some women long for spiritual intimacy. Other women are moved by watching their husband help with the laundry, invest time in the kids, and help with the dishes. Some men just want to be appreciated and long to hear, "Thanks for all your hard work." Words of appreciation and encouragement can act like an aphrodisiac. Critical and harsh words can put a wet blanket on romance. Husbands and wives are wise to study their spouse and learn what draws them close and what pushes them away.

5. What touches the green/go button inside of you when it comes to romance? What pushes the red/stop button inside of you when it comes to romance?

> Green for go . . .

> Red for stop . . .

90

CATCH UP AND READ AHEAD

Take some time today to reflect on everything that you have learned this week. If you have been doing this study section on your own, connect with your spouse and discuss some of these key insights. Use any of the following prompts to help guide this time.

- What have you been learning about what the Bible teaches about who you and your spouse are as sexual beings?
- Are there ways your perspective on romance, sexuality, and sex have changed due to this study? If so, in what ways?
- How can you and your spouse pray for each other when it comes to this important part of your lives?
- What are ways that you believe you can grow to love Jesus more and serve him with greater faithfulness if you take the care of your romantic life in marriage more seriously?

Use this time to go back and complete any of the study and reflection questions from previous days that you weren't able to finish. Make a note below of any revelations you've had and reflect on any growth or personal insights you've gained.

You may wish to review chapters 8–9 and 14 in *Sacred Marriage* before the next gathering. Make note below of anything in those chapters that stands out to you or encourages you.

WEEK 6

BEFORE GROUP MEETING	Review chapters 8–9 and 14 in Sacred Marriage Read the Welcome section (page 94)
GROUP MEETING	Discuss the Connect questions Watch the video teaching for session 6 Discuss the questions that follow as a group Do the closing exercise and pray (pages 94–98)
STUDY 1	Complete the personal (or couple) study (pages 100–102)
STUDY 2	Complete the personal (or couple) study (pages 103–105)
STUDY 3	Complete the personal (or couple) study (pages 106–108)
WRAP IT UP	Complete any unfinished personal studies (page 109) Connect with your group about the next study that you want to go through together

SESSION SIX

SACRED HISTORY

Sacred history is the gift of walking together with your spouse over the years, through joys and sorrows, and hanging in there as your hearts and minds become one. Love grows, devotion becomes reflexive, God is glorified, and we find delight in the sacred history we are making.

WELCOME | READ ON YOUR OWN

We live in a world of drive-through fast food and microwave popcorn. However, if you want great carnitas, the meat needs to be slow-cooked for hours. Baking a homemade apple pie demands a painstaking process of peeling apples, adding the right ingredients, making crust, and cooking it for just the right amount of time. But when the crust is firm and the apples are tender, there are few greater gifts to your tastebuds than taking that first warm bite. There are some culinary delights that you just can't microwave!

With our modern tech advancements, it is possible to write a love song or poem to your spouse in a matter of minutes using simple AI tools. Just pop in their name and a couple of key words like *love*, *beautiful*, *passion*, and *forever*, and your computer will do the rest. But if your beloved finds out that AI is the real poet and author, it will lose the romantic effect. On the other hand, if you spend days or weeks crafting a love poem or song, doing all you can to pour your heart and mind into this project, and your spouse knows it comes from the depth of your soul, it will be treasured for a lifetime. You just can't rush romance!

The same is true when it comes to writing sacred history. It takes *time*. In this case, years and even decades. In our modern culture, we want things now (or better yet, yesterday). But into this world of instant gratification, God whispers to us, "Hang in there. Be patient. Persevere, keep loving in the hard times, and don't give up." If we heed the voice of God, we will partner with him and our spouse to write a sacred history that is unique in all of human history.

CONNECT | 15 MINUTES

Get this session started by choosing one or both of the following questions to discuss together as a group:

- What is something that spoke to you in last week's personal study that you would like to share with the group?

— *or* —

- What are some things that should not be rushed? Why is there more satisfaction when you take the time to fully experience those things?

Session Six: Sacred History

WATCH | 20 MINUTES

Now watch the video for this session. Below is an outline of the key points covered during the teaching. Record any key concepts that stand out to you.

OUTLINE

I. A long journey that two people take together.
   A. Just starting the journey (a story).
   B. The relationship of God and his people:
   C. Season 1: Joy and celebration.
   D. Season 2: Frustration and anger.
   E. Season 3: Infidelity and apostasy.
   F. Season 4: Silence and distance.
II. The journey from me to we.
   A. How our brains work.
   B. Wrong expectations (personal history and Hollywood).
   C. Parallel journey of faith and marriage.
III. The essential place of perseverance (Luke 8:1–15).
   A. The example of freedom from addiction.
   B. Perseverance is the road to maturity (James 1:4).
   C. The same things that draw us close to God also strengthen our marriage.
   D. The surprise comparison between the honeymoon stage and a thirty-fifth anniversary.
IV. The toughest season—expect it!
   A. Research about the child-rearing years.
   B. This season is harder than you realize (a marathon story).
   C. Identifying Satan's lies (John 10:10).
   D. The fruit of perseverance (a coach's story).

NOTES

_____

_____

_____

_____

_____

_____

NOTES

Session Six: Sacred History

DISCUSS | 35 MINUTES

Discuss what you just watched by answering the following questions.

1. God's relationship with his people, the Israelites, provides an example of four distinct seasons of marriage. Each of these can be an opportunity for growth as a couple and as individuals. Talk about a time you experienced growth in one of these seasons. What did God do in your marriage and in your spiritual life?

2. Why is it important to honestly acknowledge that every marriage will have seasons of intimacy, distance, romantic bliss, and relational tension? What challenges might a couple face if they refuse to embrace that even good marriages face hard times?

3. Ask someone to read John 10:10. What are some of the lies Satan tells a husband and wife during the hard times of marriage? What is one lie you heard him whisper in your heart? How did you respond to this deceitful declaration from the enemy?

4. Talk about a marriage habit that took time for you to embrace and incorporate into your life as a couple. How did things change when this behavior became a reflexive part of your lifestyle?

5. Ask someone to read Luke 8:12–15 and James 1:2–4. Perseverance (hanging in there with tenacious resilience) is needed for a strong Christian marriage. What helps a couple persevere over time and through the challenging seasons of marriage? Where do you need to grow in perseverance as a couple? How can others pray for you and support you in your commitment to hang in there together?

RESPOND | 10 MINUTES

For most of history, due to shorter lifespans, people were with their spouses for only twenty to twenty-five years. Abraham and Sarah were together a *lot* longer, and they faced their fair share of painful moments. In our modern world, many people are living into their eighties and nineties, which means it would not be unusual for a couple to be married for five or six decades. Take a few minutes on your own or as a couple to read some of Abraham and Sarah's story (see Genesis 12; 16–18; 20–21), and then answer the following questions.

How was God with Abraham and Sarah through their long marriage?

What is a lesson you can learn from this ancient and imperfect marriage?

PRAY | 10 MINUTES

Thank God for the couples you know who have hung in there through the great times and hard times of marriage. Ask God to help you stand with your spouse and give you persevering power for the years ahead. Pray for eyes to see that God is with you in the busy times, the painful times, the frustrating times, the fruitful times, and every other time you travel together with your spouse. Finally, invite the Holy Spirit to bring lessons from this six-session study back to your mind frequently in the coming months and years ahead.

SESSION SIX

PERSONAL (OR COUPLE) STUDY

In this session, you focused on what it means to write a sacred history as a couple. Every marriage travels through seasons. Some are glorious, some painful, and some mundane. But with perseverance, prayer, and God's grace, the two can become one, and a story is written that delights God and blesses you. The key is to press through the hard times and come through on the other side more like our Savior. As you work through the exercises, write down your responses to the questions. If you are reading *Sacred Marriage* alongside this study, you might wish to first review chapters 8–9 and 14 in the book.

STUDY 1

THE JOURNEY FROM *ME* TO *WE*

Imagine an eighteen-year-old who moves out on his own. He has started trade school and is working part-time. He launches and begins a season of making his own money, decisions, and way in the world. He stays single for the next twelve and a half years. Finally, at 30.5 years of age (this is the average age a male gets married in the US), he gets married.

From the time he moved out of his parents' home, he has decided what to eat with little to no influence from anyone else. He has done this approximately 13,680 times. He has picked out his clothes, with no outside commentary, more than 4,500 times. He has decorated his apartment the way he likes, eaten what he enjoys, and gone to bed when he wanted to. He has played video games, worked lots of overtime, hung out with his friends, and done hundreds of other things, over and over, just the way he likes.

In other words, he's been single.

Now imagine the woman he is going to marry. She is 28.4 years old (the average age a woman gets married in the US). She has been on her own since she went away to college. She has asked others for advice on occasion, but for the most part she has made all the same kinds of decisions as her husband-to-be. Thousands of times over the years . . . what show to watch, who to hang out with, how to spend her free time, where to go to church.

What could possibly go wrong with these two people seeking to become one? Just have a sacred ceremony, declare vows from genuine hearts, and the two are now united in heart and mind. Boom! Slam dunk! Done! Right? Well, not so fast.

The journey of a man and a woman in the covenant of marriage—moving from *me* to *we*—is one of the most complex things in all the world. It is not easy, even when both parties love Jesus, adore each other, and are ready to give it all they have. It takes time, perseverance, humility, forgiveness, huge effort, passionate prayer, and the help of God every day.

Session Six: Sacred History

1. What were three life-history differences you brought into marriage? What impact did they make in those early days of learning to move from *me* to *we*? What is a difference that you still need to pay attention to as you are uniting your heart and life with your spouse?

Life history difference	The challenge it raises

2. If God made a movie of your marriage (short or long), what is one scene he has recorded that gives him delight and honor because you pressed through challenges and differences? How have you become more united with your spouse because of it?

There were practices and ways of thinking engrained in our minds as we grew up in our family of origin. Through our childhood years, we learned from our parents how the world works and developed ways of seeing things. Then, if we had years on our own as a single person, a new set of patterns, choices, and ways of thinking was formed. When we get married, we bring all those patterns with us, because they are imbedded in our brains. So we need to develop *new* patterns with our spouse that we do over and over again. With time, often years and in some cases decades, our way of thinking changes and our new response patterns kick in and become natural.

Sacred Marriage Bible Study

3. What is an example of a way of thinking that changed in you and helped you shift to *we* rather than *me*? How has this change in your thinking (your brain patterns) made marriage easier and more gratifying?

4. Read Philippians 4:8, Romans 12:2, and Matthew 22:37. What do you learn about your mind in these passages? Why are consistent shifts in you and your spouse's thinking essential if, as a couple, you are going to make the move from *me* to *we*?

Studies show it can take from ten to fifteen years for a couple to really become one in heart and mind. When couples give up on their marriage after five to seven years, they are missing out on the gifts God has in store for them if they will hang in there. They've dug the foundation, started to frame up the basic structure, but they don't even know what the house could look like. A good marriage isn't something you find, it's something you make. It takes a long time to grow a sense of intimate oneness.

5. If a good marriage is *not* something you find but something you make, what are some of the ways you can commit to making your marriage grow more intimate? What is something you have seen your spouse do to make your marriage improve?

STUDY 2

THE ESSENTIAL PLACE OF PERSEVERANCE

When a person learns to play guitar, it is physically painful. If someone goes to a music store and buys an acoustic guitar, it will come with strings that are made of bronze and brass. When that person plays the guitar, one of his or her hands presses down on the strings against the neck of the guitar between the frets.

The first time a person does this, it hurts. It forms a crease in the middle of the tip of each finger. With time, a guitar player who sticks with it will build up calluses, and this reduces the pain. Most non-guitar players don't know this.

Take a wild guess what percentage of people who start playing guitar last through the discomfort, build up the calluses, and finally learn to play some beautiful music. The answer is about *10 percent*. That's right—90 percent of people who pursue their dream of becoming a guitar player become guitar owners, but not players. They are simply not committed to persevere through the practice, the pain, and the weeks or months of bad-sounding efforts to play a song.

When someone gives up on his or her dream of learning to play the guitar, the price is a few weeks of sore fingers and the cost of a new or used guitar. But when someone decides to end his or her marriage, the cost is massive. Marriage calls for perseverance that far exceeds the time, effort, and pain of learning to play guitar. The pain of humble service in marriage rather than selfish demands is a lifelong pursuit. It is the way of Jesus.

The surrender of compromise and doing things in a way that works best for your spouse is a costly practice that takes *years* to become a lifestyle.

Knowing that some of the marital music does not sound perfect in those beginning years is part of the deal. But as you stay at it, practice godliness, and strive for uniting two hearts in the power of Jesus, God will amaze you by writing a sacred history that you could have never dreamed of.

◯ Sacred Marriage Bible Study

1. As you have persevered in your marriage, you are learning to count the cost and make sacrifices for your spouse, marriage, and God's glory. What are some common sacrifices all couples must make? What is one unique sacrifice you are trying to make a normative part of your marriage relationship right now?

2. Read James 1:2–4 and Luke 8:1–15 (with a focus on verse 15). How is perseverance presented as a virtue and something positive in the life of a believer? What good things does perseverance lead to, according to the Bible?

When infatuation begins to wane, our marriage will move to a whole new level of spiritual growth potential. We don't grow as much when everything is easy— the chemical boosts of infatuation push us to listen, serve, touch, give, and seek tenderness. Our spiritual growth and sense of partnership with our spouse accelerate when the infatuation wears off and we keep doing the right things day after day and year after year, even when it takes more work. This is what leads us to spiritual growth and the process of writing a sacred history with our spouse.

3. Studies of the human brain reveal it can take from ten to fifteen years for a couple to create the deepest bonds of marriage and have an enduring sense of being "one." What insights does this give you regarding the following situations?

A couple is dealing with the "seven-year itch" and wonders if the grass might be greener on the other side of the relational fence.

A husband and wife with three kids under eight who are not feeling the same romance and sizzle they had before they started a family.

Session Six: Sacred History

A married couple is celebrating their ten-year anniversary but they don't feel the level of closeness they thought they would by this point in their marriage.

4. Consider the following questions about your sacred history and record your responses. (Be sure to also talk through these questions with your spouse.)

What season are you in right now as a couple? How can God grow your life as you walk through it?

What season are you heading into as a couple? How can you prepare yourselves to stand strong as you go through this season?

Think of a couple you know who has modeled writing a sacred history. What lessons has God taught you through their example?

As you look back on challenging or painful times as a couple, how has God been present and grown you both through those seasons?

5. What are some hopes and dreams of what your future together might look like if you live each day with the awareness that you are writing a sacred history?

STUDY 3

THE HARDEST SEASON

What is the hardest point in a marathon? At what point in the 26.2-mile run do the largest number of people struggle and give up? You might think it is at the end. There are lots of clips online of people cramping up and struggling in the final stretch. But that is because most of the cameras that capture video of these events are at the finish line.

Traditionally, the toughest stretch of a marathon is between miles 18 and 20. This is when the glycogen reserves in the muscles tend to get depleted. This leads to extreme fatigue that is often accompanied by despair. Runners call this the "wall." If you hear a distance runner say, "I bonked," it means they hit the wall and had to push through massive physical, mental, and even emotional resistance to keep running.

In marriage, the point where many people tend to "bonk" is in the season when they are raising young children. This is often a time of great stress, sleep deprivation, and huge emotional demands, and the couple is still trying to figure out what it means to be married and become one with their spouse. In studies that look at marital closeness and satisfaction, this season is consistently the most challenging. When it comes to romance and intimacy, this season of marriage takes a toll on virtually every couple.

This does *not* mean couples in the child-rearing years don't have fun. It does *not* mean they can't have a rich sexual relationship. It does *not* mean they will never get time to just be a couple. What it does mean is that all of these things will take greater effort and focused intentionality. The season of raising children (particularly young children) can pull a couple apart and create discouragement and frustration—or it can bind them together as they decide to work on their relationship amid all the challenges this season naturally brings.

1. Why do you think the season of raising children is so challenging for many married couples? What can a husband and wife do in this season to keep their marriage a priority and invest intentionally in their spouse?

Session Six: Sacred History

2. Building a sacred history means hanging in there during the challenging seasons of marriage. Write down some difficulties a couple might face in *one* of the following seasons and how they can hold on to each other and to God's hand during these times:

Seasons you would love to have children but are not able to conceive . . .
Seasons when it is hard to make financial ends meet . . .
Seasons when you are raising teens and they are testing boundaries . . .
Seasons when the kids are moving out and moving on . . .

3. Think of a godly married couple you have learned from over the years. Write a note (preferably as a couple) sharing what they mean to you and how God has used their example in your life. Or, take this couple out for a cup of coffee and share what they mean in your life and how your marriage is stronger because of their example. Write down three things you have learned from this couple to share with them:

1. _____
2. _____
3. _____

Don't panic if you are not having mind-blowing sexual encounters with your spouse when you have two very young children and you are one month away from welcoming your third child into your arms. Don't question your spouse's devotion when you have kids in school, multiple sports, clubs, church activities, and you feel like the family Uber driver. Instead, in these moments, call out to God for help. Show grace to your spouse and to yourself. Start the process of writing a sacred history of patience, understanding, and selfless service.

○ Sacred Marriage Bible Study

4. In this week's group time, you heard a touching story about the letters that John Wooden would write to show his love for his wife. If someone told a story about an inspiring moment in your marriage, what might that story be?

In the tough seasons of marriage, Satan will whisper, "The future is hopeless. You married the wrong person. Time to bail out." Remember that he is a liar and the father of lies (see John 8:44). The truth is, there are seasons in which every marriage is tried in some way. You can count on it. The key is to decide in advance that you and your spouse are in it *together* for the long haul. Talk, pray, seek Jesus, find wise counsel, share your struggles with trusted Christian friends, and then pray more.

5. Take time to write a letter to your spouse expressing your commitment to writing a sacred history together through every season of your married life. Or, if writing is not your thing, do your best to express your thoughts verbally face to face or in a short video. Here are some prompts to help you in this process. (These span many seasons, some of which you may have already traveled through together. Also, not everyone will walk through all of these. Shape your message based on your unique journey.)

- ☐ I will stand (or have stood) with you through the excitement and freedom of our early years of marriage.
- ☐ I will love you (or have loved you) and tend to our marriage in the intensely busy and demanding season of babies, toddlers, and starting a family.
- ☐ I will cherish (or have cherished) you and invest in our marriage if we do not have children or struggle in the process of starting a family.
- ☐ I commit to making time for us to grow together during the season of raising a family and the challenge of the teenage years.
- ☐ I vow to keep our marriage a priority so that when the kids head out, we will still know each other and will look forward to more time together.

WRAP IT UP

Take some time today to reflect on everything that you have learned this week. If you have been doing this study section on your own, connect with your spouse and discuss some of these key insights. Use any of the following prompts to help guide this time.

- What is one truth or lesson from this session that resonated with you?
- What season are you in right now as a couple? What are the challenges and what are the joys?
- Why is it important to not get discouraged in the hard seasons of marriage?
- How have you seen movement from *me* to *we* in your years of marriage (in you, in your spouse, and as a couple)?
- How can pulling together and working as a team in the hard seasons of marriage help you write a sacred history?
- Where do you need to develop a persevering spirit in your marriage? How can you pray for this together?

Use this time to complete any of the study and reflection questions from previous days that you weren't able to finish. Make a note of any questions you've had and reflect on any growth or personal insights you've gained. Finally, discuss with your group what studies you might want to go through next and when you will plan on meeting together again to study God's Word.

LEADER'S GUIDE

Thank you for your willingness to lead your group through this study! What you have chosen to do is valuable and can make a great difference in the lives of others. The rewards and challenges of being a leader are different from those of participating in a group, and we hope that as you lead, you will discover new insights about God's plans for marriage.

Sacred Marriage is a six-session Bible study built around video content and small-group interaction. As the group leader, imagine yourself as the host of a party. Your job is to take care of your guests by managing the details so that when your guests arrive, they can focus on one another and on the interaction around the topic for that session.

Your role is not to answer all the questions or reteach the content—the video, book, and study guide will do most of that work. Your job is to guide the experience and cultivate your small group into a connected and engaged community. This will make it a place for members to process, question, and reflect—not necessarily to receive more instruction.

There are several elements in this leader's guide that will help you as you structure your study and reflection time, so be sure to follow along and take advantage of each one.

BEFORE YOU BEGIN

Before your first meeting, make sure the group members have a copy of this study guide. Alternately, you can hand out the study guides at your first meeting and give the members some time to look over the material and ask any preliminary questions. Also, make sure that the group members are aware that they have access to the streaming videos at any time by following the instructions provided with this guide. During your first meeting, ask the members to provide their names, phone numbers, and email addresses so that you can keep in touch with them over the course of the study.

Generally, the ideal size for a group is eight to ten people, which will ensure that everyone has enough time to participate in discussions. If you have more people, you might want to divide the main group into smaller subgroups. Encourage those who show up at the first meeting to commit to attending the duration of the study, as this will help the group members get to know one another, create stability for the group, and help you know how best to prepare to lead the participants through the material.

Each of the sessions in *Sacred Marriage* begins with an opening reflection in the Welcome section. The questions that follow in the Connect section serve as an icebreaker to get the group members thinking about the session topic. In the rest of the study, it's generally not a good idea to have everyone answer every question—a free-flowing discussion is more desirable. But with the icebreaker question, you can go around the circle and ask each person to respond. Encourage shy people to share, but don't force them.

At your first meeting, let the members know that each session also contains a follow-up study section they can go through on their own or—even better—with their spouses. While doing this section is optional, it will help the participants cement the concepts presented during the group study time and explore passages of Scripture related to the teaching.

Let them know that if they choose to do so, they can watch the video for the next session by accessing the streaming code provided with this study guide. Invite them to bring any questions and insights to your next meeting, especially if they had a breakthrough moment or didn't understand something.

PREPARATION FOR EACH SESSION

As the leader, there are a few things you should do to prepare for each meeting:

- **Read through the session.** This will help you become more familiar with the content and know how to structure the discussion times.

- **Decide how the videos will be used.** Determine whether you want the members to watch the videos ahead of time (again, via the streaming access code provided with this study guide) or together as a group.

- **Decide which questions you want to discuss.** Based on the length of your discussions, you may not be able to get through all the questions. So look over the discussion questions and mark which ones you definitely want to cover.

- **Be familiar with the questions you want to discuss.** When the group meets, you'll be watching the clock, so make sure you are familiar with the questions you have selected. In this way you will ensure that you have the material more deeply in your mind than your group members.

- **Pray for your group.** Pray for your group members and ask God to lead them as they study his Word and listen to his Spirit.

Keep in mind as you lead the discussion times that in many cases there will be no one "right" answer to the questions. Answers will vary, especially when the group members are being asked to share their personal experiences.

STRUCTURING THE DISCUSSION TIME

You will need to determine with your group how long you want your meetings to last so that you can plan your time accordingly. Suggested times for each section have been provided in this study guide, and if you adhere to these times, your group will meet for ninety minutes. However, many groups like to meet for two hours. If this describes your particular group, follow the times listed in the right-hand column of the chart below.

Section	90 Minutes	120 Minutes
CONNECT (discuss one or more of the opening questions for the session)	10 minutes	15 minutes
WATCH (watch the teaching material together and take notes)	25 minutes	25 minutes
DISCUSS (discuss the study questions you selected ahead of time)	35 minutes	50 minutes
RESPOND (write down key takeaways)	10 minutes	15 minutes
PRAY (pray together and dismiss)	10 minutes	15 minutes

As the group leader, it is up to you to keep track of the time and to keep things on schedule. You might want to set a timer for each segment so that both you and the group members know when the time is up. (There are some good phone apps for timers that play a gentle chime or other pleasant sound instead of a disruptive noise.)

Don't be concerned if group members are quiet or slow to share. Just ask a question, and let it hang in the air until someone shares. You can then say, "Thank you. What about others? What came to you when you watched that portion of the teaching?"

GROUP DYNAMICS

Leading a group through *Sacred Marriage* will prove to be highly rewarding. But you still may encounter challenges along the way! Discussions can get off track. Group members may not be sensitive to the needs and ideas of others. Some might worry that they will be expected to talk about matters that make them feel awkward. To help ease this strain on you and the group, consider the following ground rules:

- When someone raises a question or comment that is off the main topic, suggest you deal with it another time, or, if you feel led to go in that direction, let the group know that you will be spending some time discussing it.

- If someone asks a question you don't know how to answer, admit it and move on. At your discretion, feel free to invite group members to comment on questions that call for personal experience.

- If you find that one or two people are dominating the discussion time, direct a few questions to others in the group. Outside the main group time, ask the more dominating members to help you draw out the quieter ones. Work to make them part of the solution instead of part of the problem.

- When a disagreement occurs, encourage the group members to process the matter in love. Encourage those on opposite sides to restate what they heard the other side say about the matter, and then invite each side to evaluate if that perception is accurate. Lead the group in examining other scriptures related to the topic and look for common ground.

When any of these issues arise, encourage your group members to: "Love one another" (John 13:34), "Live at peace with everyone" (Romans 12:18), and "Be quick to listen, slow to speak and slow to become angry" (James 1:19). This will make your group time more rewarding and beneficial for everyone who attends.

Thank you again for taking the time to lead your group. You are making a difference in your group members' lives as you help them understand how they can make their marriage a *sacred marriage* and create a satisfying sacred history that will influence others.

ABOUT THE AUTHOR AND WRITERS

Gary Thomas's writing and speaking draw people closer to Christ and closer to others. He is the author of more than twenty books that together have sold more than two million copies and have been translated into more than fifteen languages. These books include *Sacred Marriage, Sacred Pathways, Cherish,* and *When to Walk Away*. Gary holds a bachelor's degree in English literature from Western Washington University, a master's degree in systematic theology from Regent College (Vancouver, BC), and an honorary doctor of divinity degree from Western Seminary (Portland, OR). He and his wife, Lisa, live in Colorado.

Dr. Kevin G. Harney is the president and co-founder of Organic Outreach International and the teaching pastor of Shoreline Church in Monterey, California. He is the author of the *Organic Outreach* trilogy, *Organic Disciples*, more than one hundred small group guides, and numerous articles. He does extensive teaching and speaking nationally and internationally to equip leaders in effective and culture-changing discipleship and evangelism.

Sherry Harney is the co-founder of Organic Outreach International and is the spiritual development director at Shoreline Church in Monterey, California. She is the author of *Organic Prayer,* co-author of the *Organic Outreach* trilogy, *Organic Disciples*, and has written more than one hundred small group guides with writers such as Ann Voskamp, Max Lucado, Christine Caine, N.T. Wright, Dallas Willard and others. Sherry speaks for national and international groups with a focus on prayer, discipleship, and natural evangelism.

Kevin and Sherry have three married sons, three daughters-in-law, and five grandchildren.

OTHER BIBLE STUDIES FROM
GARY THOMAS

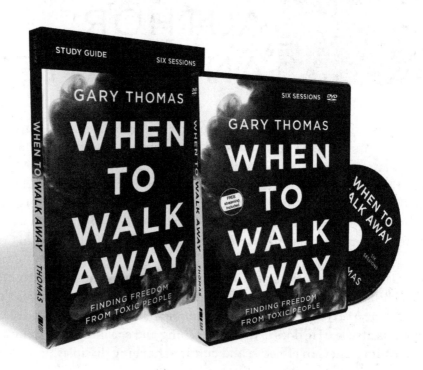

AVAILABLE WHEREVER BOOKS ARE SOLD.

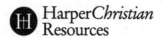

ALSO AVAILABLE FROM
GARY THOMAS

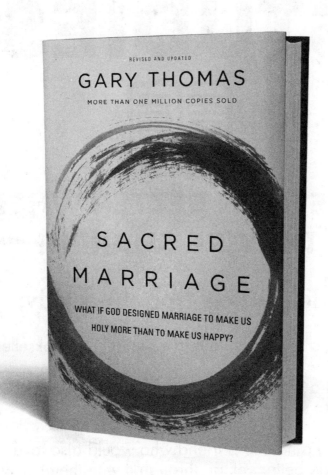

AVAILABLE WHEREVER BOOKS ARE SOLD.

From the Publisher

GREAT STUDIES

ARE EVEN BETTER WHEN THEY'RE SHARED!

Help others find this study:

- Post a review at your favorite online bookseller.

- Post a picture on a social media account and share why you enjoyed it.

- Send a note to a friend who would also love it—or, better yet, go through it with them!

Thanks for helping others grow their faith!